See the
Wider picture

Hot air balloons and cave houses, Cappadocia, central Turkey

These strange rocks are millions of years old. The weather has made them this way. They look incredible from the air which is why Cappadocia is a popular place for hot air balloons.

Can you see a cave in the mountain? Today, people still live in these caves which were built thousands of years ago.

Would you like to live in a cave?

Pearson Education Limited
KAO TWO, KAO Park
Hockham Way, Harlow
Essex, CM17 9SR, England
and Associated Companies throughout the world

www.pearsonenglish.com

First published 2018
Eleventh impression 2022
ISBN: 978-1-292-17883-7

Set in Harmonia Sans
Printed in Slovakia by Neografia

Acknowledgements

The Publishers would like to thank all the teachers and students around the world who contributed to the development of Wider World, especially the teachers on the Wider World Teacher Advisory Panel: Irina Alyapysheva, CEE; Reyna Arango, Mexico; Marisa Ariza, Spain; Alfredo Bilopolski, Argentina; Isabel Blecua, Spain; Camilo Elcio de Souza, Brazil; Ingrith del Carmen Ríos Verdugo, Mexico; Edward Duval, Belgium; Norma González, Argentina; Natividad Gracia, Spain; Claribel Guzmán, Mexico; Izabela Lipińska, Poland; Fabián Loza, Mexico; Miguel Mozo, Spain; Huỳnh Thᴺ Ái Nguyên, Vietnam; Joacyr Oliveira, Brazil; Montse Priego, Spain; Gladys Rodriguez, Argentina; Lyudmila Slastnova, CEE; Izabela Stępniewska, Poland.
The Publishers would also like to thank the teachers who contributed to the Go Getter series, as materials from Go Getter Level 1 were adapted to create Wider World Starter Level.
Anna Borek, CEE; Svetlana Chistyakova, CEE; Marina Grechanichenko, CEE; Sofija Ljilak Vukajlovič, CEE; Ece Kahraman, Turkey; Maria Soledad Saravai O'Keefe, Argentina; Bilbana Pavolvič, CEE; Jovana Popovič, CEE; Alla Sichurova, CEE; Marta Skałbania, CEE; Anna Standish, CEE; Katarzyna Szwejkowska, CEE; Renata Woldan, CEE; Ewa Wódkówska, CEE; Oksana Zinchenko, CEE.

Photo Acknowledgements

The Publishers would like to thank the following for their kind permission to reproduce their photographs:

123RF.com: 23, 32, 34, 38, 4, 43, 7, 7, 72, 72, 74, 78, 8, 5second 74, Adrian Ilie 83, Antonio Guillem 22, Danila Krylov 36, Elena Petrova 3, Eric Isselee 77, 77, Erik Lam 40, Everett B Palmer IV 4, Georgii Dolgykh 6, Iakov Filimonov 53, Igor Kovalchuk 73, Igor Plotnikov 57, Iuliia Sokolovska 74, Kwanchai Chai-udom 83, Marco Salomon 54, Marin Conic 48, Michael Simons 48, NejroN 74, Oleksandr Grybanov 54, Olena Mykhaylova 62, Olesia Bilkei 72, Pan Xunbin 71, Pauliene Wessel 34, Photodeti 72, Piotr Adamowicz 48, Richard Thomas 6, Ruslan Gilmanshin 34, Sergei Uriadnikov 87, Sergey Lavrentev 54, Sergey Novikov 24, 86, StockedHouseStudio 56, Suttipon Yakham 77, Tatiana Shevchenko 83, Uladzimir MARTYSHKIN 19, Valentyna Chukhlyebova 74, Valentyna Zhukova 87, Valery Voennyy 48, Vichaya Kiatying-Angsulee 62, Viparat Kluengsuwanchai 57, Vitaly Korovin 6, Waldemar Dabrowski 77, Wang Aizhong 74, Yulia Remezova 27, aberration 54, amarosy 27, angel_a 37, balefire9 39, belchonock 54, 57, believeinme33 12, claudiodivizia 57, damedeeso 69, deusexlupus 78, ferli 86, indigolotos 18, isselee 43, jackf 17, khvost 18, krasnoyarsk 16, luchschen 57, magone 6, mavoimage 27, mikelane45 56, monticello 6, nerthuz 78, nikolaich 48, okan akdeniz 34, piko72 71, saphira 57, scyther5 4, snake3d 7, spotmatikphoto 86, stefanschurr 56, tarzhanova 27, tim2infinity 57, vilainecrevette 74, whiskybottle 37, willyambradberry 56, wuttichok panichiwarapun 36; **Alamy Stock Photo:** Art Collection 2 14, Blend Images 24, ChiccoDodiFC 52, Heritage Image Partnership Ltd 14, Image Source Plus 86, Myrleen Pearson 37, North Wind Picture Archives 14, RTimages 12, Sergey Novikov 86, Zoonar GmbH 86, dieKleinert 14, **Datacraft Co Ltd:** 38;

Fotolia: BGodunoff 28, Dmitry Naumov 32, MNStudio 16, Tatty 28, georgerudy 13, 13, pink candy 13, sonne_fleckl 12, venusangel 36; **Getty Images:** Bettmann 14, Donald Maclellan/Hulton Archive 14, Hero Images 12, Jay Blakesbert/UpperCut Images 47, Juice Images/Cultura 8, Sidekick 26, jabejon/iStock 27; **Pearson Education Asia Ltd:** Cheuk-king Lo 6; **Pearson Education Ltd:** Gareth Boden 38, Jon Barlow 21, 22, 22, 23, 29, 37, 39, 39, 4, 4, 4, 4, 49, 49, 49, 49, 49, 79, 79, 79, 79, 9, 9, Jules Selmes 37, Studio 8 22; **Shutterstock.com:** Aaron Amat 43, Africa Studio 62, Aleksandr Kurganov 23, Aleksey Stemmer 74, Alena Ozerova 40, Andrienko Anastasiya 39, Anitham Raju Yaragorla 74, Ann Baldwin 7, Atiketta Sangasaeng 36, Baloncici 32, Bildagentur Zoonar GmbH 74, Blend Images 24, BonD80 23, Boris Rabtsevich 12, Catalin Petolea 42, Chintla 32, Chiyacat 27, Christophe Testi 10, 14, 17, Craig Wactor 82, Cultura Motion 34, Dean Drobot 16, Deborah Kolb 24, Denis Radovanovic 22, DenisNata 19, Ditty_about_summer 56, Dja65 34, Dmitry Kalinovsky 73, Dudarev Mikhail 48, Dusan Zidar 40, Ekaterina V. Borisova 77, Elena Elisseeva 82, Elnur 18, 48, Eric Isselee 27, 27, 77, Everything 19, Ewelina Wachala 37, 37, Fh Photo 37, Fotofermer 71, Fotogroove 10, 14, 17, Four Oaks 57, Gelpi 47, 60, Globe Turner 10, Golbay 18, Gunnar Pippel 72, Hefr 74, Herschel Hoffmeyer 57, Hintau Aliaksei 74, Hong Vo 27, IdeaStudio 40, Igor Sokolov 78, Jacek Bieniek 19, Johan Larson 72, Johannes Kornelius 32, Justina.au 74, Karkas 18, 18, KateStone 27, Kesu 72, Kiril Stanchev 16, Kiselev Andrey Valerevich 42, 48, Lucy Liu 18, MAHATHIR MOHD YASIN 63, MSPhotographic 19, Marco Mayer 32, MariyanaM 71, Mark Herreid 62, Media Guru 32, Melica 54, Michael Kraus 34, Mikadun 37, Mike Flippo 19, 56, Mike Pellinni 7, Mirek Kijewski 77, Monkey Business Images 40, 82, Nata-Lia 23, Nestor Noci 62, Nording 78, OZaiachin 32, Oleksiy Mark 23, Olga Popova 27, 39, 39, Omsickova Tatyana 40, Paul Stringer 10, 14, Phant 7, PhotoNAN 19, Photobankgallery 81, Raisa Kanareva 42, SFROLOV 67, Samuel Borges Photography 62, Sashkin 71, SekarB 87, Sergey Peterman 42, Sergii Korshun 38, Sergiy Kuzmin 12, ShutterStockStudio 62, Siberia Video and Photo 42, Sklep Spozywczy 27, Stuart Monk 37, StudioSmart 36, StudioSmile 6, Studiotouch 7, Taiftin 19, Tony_C 18, Tracy Starr 87, Tracy Whiteside 24, Tristan Tan 43, Tyler Hartl 7, Tyler Olson 16, 48, Utekhina Anna 73, VaLiza 63, Vincent St. Thomas 6, Vladimir Mucibabic 52, W. Scott McGill 34, YK 36, Yeko Photo Studio 34, altanaka 40, arapix 19, arka38 27, bloom 19, caimacanul 6, cbpix 72, charnsitr 10, 14, defpicture 39, dien 73, ekler 10, 14, elRoce 57, goodluz 40, gt29 4, hanzl 78, imagefactory 34, kanate 7, kavring 7, lewald 74, mashe 82, movit 12, naluwan 42, nattanan726 43, nikshor 7, nogandosan 62, oksana2010 6, pun photo 6, rattanapatphoto 39, rzymuR 27, sanneberg 82, smuay 28, topseller 82, virtu studio 48, wavebreakmedia 16.
Cover Images: *Front:* **Alamy Stock Photo:** imageBROKER

Illustration Acknowledgements

Joanna Bernat (Pigeon) p. 11, 28, 29, 38, 42, 48, 58, 59, 66 ; Ewa Ciałowicz (Pigeon) p. 49, 53, 56, 68, 78, 80; Michał Domański (Pigeon) p. 23, 24 (line characters), 32, 33, 34, 36, 84; Alicja Gapińska pp 9, 10, 14, 18, 19, 21, 24, 29, 31, 38, 41, 51, 59, 75, 81; Matylda Kozera (Pigeon) p. 68 ; Beata Krajewska (Studio Gardengraf) p. 8, 53; Daniel Limon (Beehive Illustration) p. 44, 64, 79; Adam Linley (Beehive Illustration) p. 24 (crossword clues), 68 (butterfly); Jim Peacock (Beehive Illustration) p. 14, 52; Alan Rowe p. 5, 10, 20, 30, 40, 50, 60, 70, 80; Marcin Rutkowski (Pigeon) p. 19, 28; Matijos Gebreselassie (Pigeon) p. 22.

Every effort has been made to trace the copyright holders and we apologise in advance for any unintentional omissions. We would be pleased to insert the appropriate acknowledgement in any subsequent edition of this publication.

CONTENTS

0 Get Started!

I can say and spell my name.

VOCABULARY
Numbers | Colours | Classroom objects

GRAMMAR
Spelling | Singular and plural

COMMUNICATION
Classroom instructions

1 Label the photos with the names below.

~~Alex~~   Jen   Lian   Lucas

1   _Alex_   2 _____   3 _____   4 _____

2 Label the photos with the words below.

computer   ~~computer game~~   Maths   music

1   _computer game_   2 _____   3 _____   4 _____

3 Look and complete the sentences.

Hi. I'm Alex. I [1] _like_ computers and computer [2] g a m e s!

Hello. [3] _'_ Jen. I like [4] c _____ s!

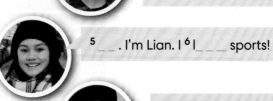
[5] _ _ . I'm Lian. I [6] l _ _ _ sports!

[7] _____ . I'm Lucas. I like [8] m _ _ _ _ _ and Maths!

4 Complete the alphabet.

A   B   [1]C   D   [2]_   F   G

[3]_   I   J   K   [4]_   M   [5]_

O   P   [6]_   R   [7]_   T

U   [8]_   W   X   [9]_   Z

5 Complete the words with the letters below.

b   f   g   l   s   t

1   _l_ion
2   _ish
3   _andwich
4   _able
5   _irl
6   _oy

6 Match 1–5 to a–e.

1   What's your [b]
2   My name's ☐
3   How do you ☐
4   I'm twelve ☐
5   I'm from ☐

a   Bernadette.
b   name?
c   Spain.
d   spell your name?
e   years old.

4

0.2 NUMBERS and COLOURS

I can say numbers 1-20 and name basic colours.

1 Put the words in the correct order to make sentences.

1 Superdug / also / Dug / is / .
Dug is also Superdug.

2 is / superhero / He / a / .

_____

3 Kit / Dug's / friend / is / .

_____

4 clever / She / is / very / .

_____

2 Write the numbers.

five	twelve	one	ten
5	☐	☐	☐
eight	four	eleven	six
☐	☐	☐	☐
three	seven	nine	six
☐	☐	☐	☐

3 Complete the missing numbers.

two   four   ¹*six*   eight   ten   ²_____
one   three   ³_____   seven   ⁴_____   eleven

4 Write the numbers.

1	eleven	*11*	6	seventeen	_____
2	fourteen	_____	7	twenty	_____
3	nineteen	_____	8	thirteen	_____
4	fifteen	_____	9	sixteen	_____
5	twelve	_____	10	eighteen	_____

5 Match colours 1-6 to the words.

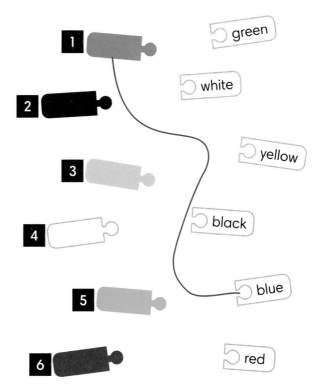

green
white
yellow
black
blue
red

6 Look at the box and write the colours.

five	eleven	~~four~~	sixteen
twelve	twenty	**nineteen**	
eight	thirteen	seventeen	

1	4	*red*	6	5	_____
2	12	_____	7	17	_____
3	16	_____	8	19	_____
4	11	_____	9	20	_____
5	13	_____	10	8	_____

I can talk about classroom objects and understand classroom instructions.

1 Circle the correct word.

1   sandwich / (book)   2   pencil / pen

3   notebook / ruler   4   bag / sandwich

5   pen / pencil   6   notebook / ruler

2 Write the plural.

1	a pencil	three	_pencils_
2	a book	nine	_____
3	a sandwich	ten	_____
4	a pencil	ten	_____
5	a notebook	five	_____
6	a pen	seven	_____
7	a box	thirteen	_____
8	a ruler	eleven	_____
9	a table	two	_____
10	a cupcake	six	_____

3 Complete with *It's* or *They're*.

1   _It's_ a bin.   4   _____ a desk.
2   _____ clocks.   5   _____ chairs.
3   _____ a   6   _____ bins.
    board.

4 Find and circle five words in the wordsnake.
Then label the classroom objects.

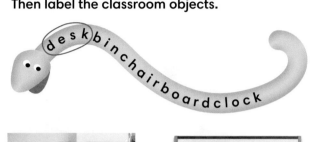

1 *desk*   2 _____

3 _____   4 _____

5 _____

5 Read the expressions. Who usually says them?
Circle T (teacher) or S (student)

1   Open your books.   (T)/ S
2   Can you help me, please?   T / S
3   Stand up.   T / S
4   Work in pairs.   T / S
5   What's … in English?   T / S
6   Write your name.   T / S

6 Put the dialogue in the correct order.

a ☐ Can you repeat that, please?
b ☐ What does *brilliant* mean?
c ☐ It means very good.
d ☐ 1 Hello, Mrs Gold. Can you help me, please?
e ☐ Yes, Tom. How can I help?
f ☐ Yes. It means *very good*.

0.4 SELF-CHECK

Vocabulary

1 Circle the correct answer.

0	thirteen	(13)/ 11
1	twelve	20 / 12
2	seventeen	17 / 15
3	●	blue / green
4	●	red / yellow
5	●	black / white

/5

2 Look at the photos and write the words.

0 *pen*

1 _____

2 _____

3 _____

4 _____

5 _____

Grammar

3 Circle the correct words.

0 (It's a)/ They're cupcake.
1 It's a / They're tables.
2 It's a / They're zebra.
3 It's a / They're desks.
4 It's a / They're elephants.
5 It's a / They're flower.

/5

4 Complete with the plural form of the words.

0 eight *pencils* (pencil)

1 six _____ (book)

2 two _____ (box)

3 three _____ (bin)

4 two _____ (sandwich)

5 four _____ (tree)

/5

Communication

5 Complete the sentences with the words below.

books   down   ~~help~~   pairs   please   up

Can you ⁰ *help* me, ¹ _____ ?

Sit ² _____ .

Close your ³ _____ .

Work in ⁴ _____ .

Stand ⁵ _____ .

/5

Vocabulary	/10
Grammar	/10
Communication	/5
Your total score	/25

1

Family and friends

I can talk about the people in a family.

1 Who is who in Sally's family? Match a–g to 1–7.

1	Sally's father	**b**
2	Sally's mother	☐
3	Sally's parents	☐ ☐
4	Sally's grandfather	☐
5	Sally's grandmother	☐
6	Sally's brothers	☐ ☐
7	Sally's sister	☐

2 Match the word fragments to make family words.

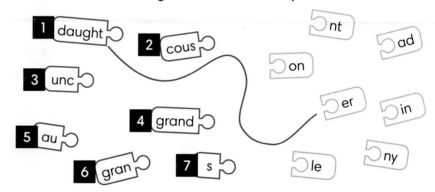

1 daught
2 cous
3 unc
4 grand
5 au
6 gran
7 s

nt
ad
on
er
in
ny
le

3 Look at Mark's family tree. Complete the sentences with one word.

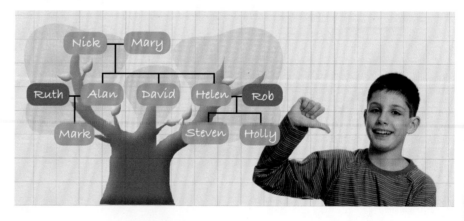

1 Alan: Nick is my ¹*father*. He's Mark's ² _____ . too.
2 Holly: Ruth is my ³ _____ . Steven and I are Mark's ⁴ _____ .
   I am Helen and Rob's ⁵ _____ .
3 Steven: Holly is my ⁶ _____ . I'm Helen's ⁷ _____ .

4 Read and complete.
1 Amy is Emily's mother. Emily is Amy's **daughter**.
2 Tom is Danny's father. Danny is Tom's _____ .
3 Sara is Ben's mother and Ted's aunt. Ben and Ted are _____ .
4 Ada is Sam's mother. Sam is Rosa's father. Ada is Rosa's _____ .
5 John is David's brother. David is Tina's father. John is Tina's _____ .

GRAMMAR *to be* affirmative

I can use the affirmative form of the verb *to be*, *my* and *your*.

1 Look at the pictures. Circle the correct word.

A birthday party

1 Look. We *am* / *are* / *is* at Tom's house.

2 Tom *am* / *are* / *is* twelve today.

3 I *am* / *are* / *is* happy!

A new student

4 He *am* / *are* / *is* a teacher.

5 She *am* / *are* / *is* a student.

6 They *am* / *are* / *is* in the classroom.

7 You *am* / *are* / *is* in this classroom.

2 Look at Exercise 1. Complete the sentences using short forms of the verb *to be*.

1 Look. We're at Tom's house.

2 Tom _____ twelve today.

3 I _____ happy!

4 He _____ a teacher.

5 She _____ a student.

6 They _____ in the classroom.

7 You _____ in this classroom.

3 Complete the dialogue with *am*, *are* or *is*.

Harry: Hi. I ¹**am** Harry.

Jack: Hi, Harry. I ²_____ Jack. You ³_____ in Class 2 with me. Welcome!

Harry: Thanks.

Jack: This is Tony. He ⁴_____ my classmate. We ⁵_____ best friends too. Mrs Lee and Mr Brown ⁶_____ my favourite teachers.

4 Complete with *my* or *your*.

This is ¹_____ Granny, Sophie.

This is ²_____ present, Granny.

5 Complete the sentences with the words below.

| ~~am~~ are is my They |

Hi! I ¹**am** Tom. This is ²_____ family. My parents' names ³_____ Amy and Andrew. ⁴_____ are teachers. My sister ⁵_____ thirteen.

1.3 GRAMMAR   *to be* negative

I can talk about countries and nationalities and use the negative form of the verb *to be*.

1 Rewrite the sentences. Use the short forms of the verb *to be*.

1 My friends are not in the classroom.
   My friends aren't in the classroom.

2 You are not right.
   _____

3 I am not a superhero.
   _____

4 Ben is not my friend.
   _____

5 She is not my aunt.
   _____

6 They are not my cousins.
   _____

2 Write negative sentences. Use the short forms of the verb *to be*.

1 She's eleven. She's in the classroom.
   She isn't eleven.
   She _____ .

2 They're happy. They're in the house.
   They _____ .

3 He's a teacher. He's ready for school.
   He _____ .
   _____ . He _____ .
   _____ .

3 VOCABULARY Complete the words and write the nationalities.

1   P o l a n d   *Polish*

2   F _ _ _ _ _ e   _____

3   the _ _   _____

4   T _ _ _ _ _ y   _____

5   C _ _ _ a   _____

6 the _ _ _ _   _____

7 S _ _ _ n   _____

4 Write sentences that are true for you. Write *am*, *'m not*, *are*, *aren't*, *is* or *isn't*.

1 My school *is / isn't* in the USA.

2 My English teacher _____ British.

3 My friends _____ in China.

4 My parents _____ Polish.

5 I _____ Turkish.

6 I _____ twelve.

5 Complete the dialogue with the verb *to be*. Use an affirmative form (✓) or a negative form (✗).

Kit: It ¹*is* (✓) you, Dug! You ²_____ (✓) with your grandad and granny, right?

Dug: No, I ³_____ (✗). They ⁴_____ (✓) my parents. My dad ⁵_____ (✓) British, but my mother ⁶_____ (✗) British. She ⁷_____ (✓) Polish.

Kit: It ⁸_____ (✗) a new photo.

Dug: That's right. The photo ⁹_____ (✓) very old.

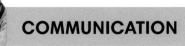
I can make introductions.

🔊 **02** Introductions.

A: *Mum*, **this is** *Lucas.*
     He is my *friend/classmate.*
     Lucas, **this is my mum.**
B: **Hello,** *Lucas.* **Nice to meet you.**
C: **Nice to meet you too.**

1 Complete the dialogues.

Hi, Jill.

1 **b**
2 ☐

1 a   Sorry, Mum!
   b   Hi, Mum!
   c   It's OK, Mum!

2 a   This is Amy.
   b   I'm Amy.
   c   You are here, Amy.

Amy is my new classmate

3 ☐
4 ☐

3 a   You're Amy.
   b   Hello, Amy.
   c   Thank you, Amy.

4 a   Nice to meet you, Jill.
   b   Nice to meet you, Mrs Wilson.
   c   Nice to meet you, Amy.

2 Complete the dialogue with the words below.

He's   Hi   Nice   ~~this is~~   to meet you

Thomas: Hi, Stella, ¹*this is* Frankie. ²_____
          my cousin.
Stella: ³_____, Frankie. Nice ⁴_____.
Frankie: ⁵_____ to meet you too, Stella.

3 Complete the dialogue with sentences a–d.

May: ¹**b**
Auntie Sue: Oh, hello, May!
May: And this is Nancy. ²___
Auntie Sue: Hello, Nancy. ³___
Nancy: Hello, Mrs Smith. ⁴___

a   She's my best friend at school.
b   Hi, Auntie Sue.
c   Nice to meet you.
d   Nice to meet you too.

4 Write a dialogue like in Exercise 3. Introduce your English friend to your teacher.

You: _____
Teacher: _____
You: _____
              _____
Your friend: _____
Teacher: _____

I can understand a text about family photos and places.

My photo album

A

2 ☐
This is my friend Bea. She's in the park. Her mum is Turkish and her dad is British. She's fun. Sweep is in the photo too. He's Bea's dog.

C

1 ☐
In this photo, my mum and dad are with Aunt Ellie. They aren't at home, they're on holiday in Spain. They are happy. Aunt Ellie is my dad's sister. My dad's family is Spanish.

B

3 ☐
Hi. I'm Silvia and this is my brother, Nick. I'm fourteen and he's ten. We're from Manchester. It's in the UK.

1 Read the texts. Match texts 1–3 to photos A–C.

2 Read the texts again. Match 1–6 to a–f.

1 Hi. My name's   `c`
2 I'm   ☐
3 My brother is   ☐
4 Ellie is   ☐
5 Bea is   ☐
6 Sweep is   ☐

a my aunt.
b my friend.
c Silvia.
d 14/fourteen.
e a dog.
f 10/ten.

3 Complete the sentences with *British*, *Turkish* or *Spanish*. Check your answers in the texts.

1 Silvia is *British*.
2 Nick is _____.
3 Silvia's dad is _____.
4 Aunt Ellie is _____.
5 Bea's mother is _____.
6 Bea's father is _____.

4 VOCABULARY   Look at the photos and complete the words.

1 I'm at h _ _ _ today.

2 We aren't at s _ _ _ _ _ _ today.

3 My cousins are on h _ _ _ _ _ _ _.

4 My granny and my grandad are in the p _ _ _ _.

LISTENING and WRITING | Best friends

I can understand short spoken texts and write short texts about best friends.

1 🔊 03 Read and listen. Circle T (true) or F (false).

1

1	Rob and Victor are best friends.	T / F
2	They're at Rob's house.	T / F
3	Rob's mum and Victor's mum are best friends.	T / F

2

4	Rob's on holiday.	T / F
5	Rob and Mel are in the UK.	T / F
6	Rob and Mel are cousins.	T / F

2 🔊 04 Listen again. Complete the tables.

	Rob
Age	12
Nationality	

	Victor
Age	
Nationality	

	Mel
Age	
Nationality	

3 Correct the text. Add capital letters.

Clara
~~clara~~ and ada are best friends. clara is twelve and ada is thirteen. clara is from the uk. she's british. ada is from turkey. she's turkish.

4 Read the text in Exercise 3 again. Complete the table.

	Clara	Ada
Age	12	
Country		
Nationality		

5 Look at the information and write about Pierre and Pedro.

	Pierre	Pedro
Age	12	11
Country	France	Spain
Nationality	French	Spanish

Pierre and Pedro are best friends.

Pierre is _____

_____

_____

_____

_____

_____

_____

_____

_____

I can talk and write about families in paintings.

1 Look at the painting and the people. Match the people 1–6 to the words a–f in the painting.

1 Alberto _a_

2 Rosanna

3 Stefano

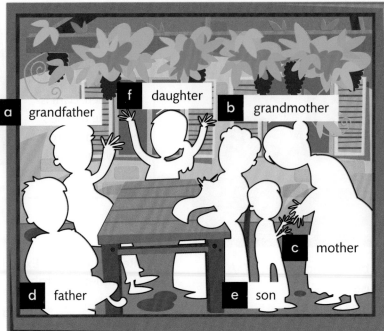

f daughter

a grandfather

b grandmother

c mother

d father

e son

4 Anna

5 Luca

6 Maria

2 Look at Exercise 1 and do the crossword puzzle.

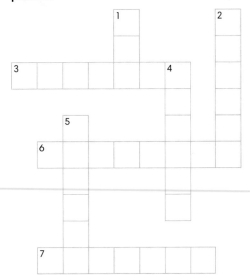

Across
3 Alberto and Maria are Stefano's _____.
6 Rosanna is Anna and Stefano's _____.
7 Luca is Rosanna's _____.

Down
1 Stefano is Maria's _____.
2 Maria is Stefano's _____.
4 Rosanna is Luca's _____.
5 Stefano is Luca's _____.

3 What nationality are the artists? Complete the sentences.

1 Leonardo da Vinci is an I t _a_ l _i_ _a_ n artist.

2 Paul Cezanne is a F _ _ _ _ c h artist.

3 David Hockney is a B _ i t _ _ _ artist.

4 Shen Zhou is a C _ i n _ _ e artist.

5 Pablo Picasso is a S _ a n _ _ _ artist.

6 Georgia O'Keeffe is an Am _ _ _ _ _ an artist.

1.8

SELF-ASSESSMENT

For each learning objective, tick (✓) the box that best matches your ability.

☺☺ = I understand and can help a friend.   ☹ = I understand but have some questions.

☺ = I understand and can do it by myself.   ☹☹ = I do not understand.

		☺☺	☺	☹	☹☹	Need help?	Now try ...
1.1	Vocabulary					Students' Book pp. 10–11 Workbook p. 8	Ex. 1–2, p. 16
1.2	Grammar					Students' Book pp. 12–13 Workbook p. 9	Ex. 3, p. 16
1.3	Grammar					Students' Book pp. 14–15 Workbook p. 10	Ex. 4, p. 16
1.4	Communication					Students' Book p. 16 Workbook p. 11	Ex. 5, p. 16
1.5	Reading and Vocabulary					Students' Book p. 17 Workbook p. 12	
1.6	Listening and Writing					Students' Book p. 18 Workbook p. 13	
1.7	CLIL					Students' Book p. 19 Workbook p. 14	

1.1   I can talk about the people in a family.
1.2   I can use the affirmative form of the verb *to be*, *my* and *your*.
1.3   I can talk about countries and nationalities and use the negative form of the verb *to be*.
1.4   I can make introductions.
1.5   I can understand a text about a family photo.
1.6   I can understand short spoken texts about best friends.
1.7   I can talk and write about families in paintings.

What can you remember from this unit?

New words I learned (the words you most want to remember from this unit)	**Expressions and phrases I liked** (any expressions or phrases you think sound nice, useful or funny)	**English I heard or read outside class** (e.g. from websites, books, adverts, films, music)

Vocabulary

1 Complete the pairs.

0   mum and *dad*

1   _____ and uncle

2   mother and _____

3   _____ and sister

4   son and _____

5   _____ and grandad

☐ /5

2 Look and complete the words.

0   She's from P o l a n d.

1   He's in the p _ _ _ _ .

2   She's A _ _ _ _ _ _ _ _ .

3   They're at s _ _ _ _ _ _ .

4   Paris is in F _ _ _ _ _ .

5   She's at h _ _ _ _ .

☐ /5

Grammar

3 Complete the sentences with the verb *to be*. Use an affirmative form (✓) or a negative form (✗).

0   This *isn't* (✗) my garden. It's a park!

1   My best friends _____ (✓) Yasemin and Jane.

2   Yasemin _____ (✓) Turkish.

3   Jane and I _____ (✗) Turkish.

4   We _____ (✓) from the UK.

5   I _____ (✗) in the UK in this photo!

☐ /5

4 Circle the correct answer.

Jack: **⁰I**/ *You* am Jack and this is ¹*my* / *your* cousin Ben. ²*They* / *We* are with Freddie. Freddie is ³*Ben* / *Ben's* dog.

Jack: Clara, you are with ⁴*my* / *your* friend Nadia in this picture, right?

Clara: Yes. Mum and ⁵*Nadia* / *Nadia's* mum are in the picture too.

☐ /5

Communication

5 Complete the dialogue with one word in each gap.

A: Jack, ⁰*this* ¹_____ my friend, Harry.

B: ²_____, Harry. ³_____ to meet you.

C: Hi, Jack. Nice to ⁴_____ you ⁵_____.

☐ /5

Vocabulary	☐ /10
Grammar	☐ /10
Communication	☐ /5
Your total score	☐ /25

1 Look at the flags and write the countries.

1   the U _ _

2   C _ n _ d _

3   I r _ l _ n d

4   N e _   Z e a _ a _ _ _

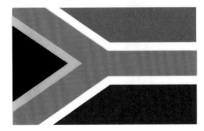

5   S o u _ _   A _ _ i _ a

6   A _ s _ r _ l _ a

2 Circle the correct answer.

Quiz

1   The capital of the UK is **_b_** .
   a   England   **b**   London   **c**   Scotland

2   There are _____ million people in the UK.
   a   650   **b**   56   **c**   65

3   There are _____ countries in the UK.
   a   two   **b**   three   **c**   four

4   The capital of the USA is _____ .
   a   Washington, DC.   **b**   New York   **c**   America

5   There are _____ million people in the USA.
   a   324   **b**   432   **c**   395

6   There are 24 million people in _____ .
   a   New Zealand   **b**   Australia   **c**   Sydney

7   The capital of Australia is _____ .
   a   Sydney   **b**   Washington, DC   **c**   Canberra

3 Look at Queen Elizabeth's family tree. Write the names.

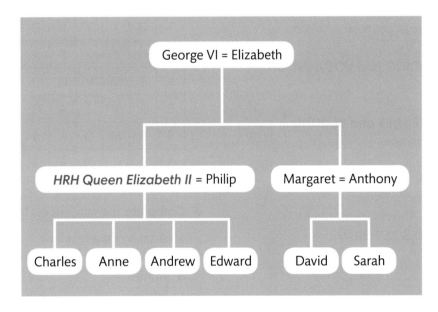

1   Queen Elizabeth's mother: _Elizabeth_
2   Edward and Andrew's uncle: _____
3   Margaret's father: _____
4   Andrew's brothers: _____ and _____
5   Sarah's aunt: _____
6   Margaret's daughter: _____
7   Charles' sister: _____
8   Anthony's son: _____
9   David and Sarah's cousins:
   _____ , _____ , _____ and
   _____
10   Sarah's uncle: _____

I can talk about clothes.

Clothes for kids

1 *trainers*   2 _____   3 _____   4 _____

1 Label photos 1–4 with the words below.

| dress   jeans   skirt   ~~trainers~~

2 Find and circle nine clothes words. Then complete the words.

T	T	R	A	C	K	S	U	I	T
E	H	B	W	Q	L	W	T	F	D
L	T	V	I	H	S	H	O	E	S
R	R	B	U	E	S	Y	P	U	S
Y	O	I	Y	R	C	L	T	B	K
D	U	T	F	F	A	E	U	X	I
R	S	M	V	C	P	C	G	Q	R
E	E	I	J	A	C	K	E	T	T
S	R	M	Q	W	S	N	Q	D	P
S	S	C	O	A	T	F	I	S	Y

1 t r a c k s u i t
2 s _ _ _ _ s
3 j _ _ _ _ t
4 c _ _ t
5 d _ _ _ _ s
6 t _ _ _ _ _ _ _ s
7 c _ p
8 t _ p
9 s _ _ _ t

3 Complete the sentences. Use the words in Exercises 1 and 2.

1 Anne's *dress* is yellow.
2 Anne's _____ is green.
3 Anne's _____ are black.
4 Eddie's _____ is blue.
5 Eddie's_____ is red.
6 Eddie's_____ are black.
7 Eddie's_____ are white.

Anne   Eddie

4 What are they? Label photos 1–4.

1 *cap*   2 _____   3 _____   4 _____

2

My things

VOCABULARY
Clothes

GRAMMAR
this, that, these, those | adjectives:
too big/small | *to be* questions and
short answers

COMMUNICATION
Asking for personal information

READING and VOCABULARY
My things

LISTENING and WRITING
Punctuation

CLIL
Geometry: Shapes

SKILLS REVISION
1 & 2

GRAMMAR   *this, that, these, those*; and adjectives

I can use *this, that, these, those* and adjectives.

1 Complete the sentences with *This*, *That*, *These* or *Those*.

1   *That* is Alex's bag.

2   _____ is my dad's bag.

3   _____ shoes are my mum's.

4   _____ shoes are Jen's.

5   _____ dress is Jen's.

6   _____ is my mum's dress.

2 **VOCABULARY** Label the pictures with the words below.

| big   ~~boring~~   cool   long   new   old   short   small

1   *boring* and _____

2   _____ and _____

3   _____ and _____

4   _____ and _____

3 Complete the sentences with *is/are*, *too* and adjectives in Exercise 2.

1   John's cap *is too small*.
2   John's jeans _____.
3   John's T-shirt _____.
4   John's trainers _____.

4 Look at the photos and write sentences. Use the words below and *this, that, these* or *those*.

| ~~a boring cap~~   an old trainer   new trousers small shoes

1   *This is a boring cap.*
2   _____
3   _____
4   _____

GRAMMAR   *to be* questions and short answers

I can ask and answer questions with the verb *to be*.

1 Add a question mark (?) or a full stop (.).

1 Is he French   `?`
2 My brother is eight years old   ☐
3 Are you a student   ☐
4 Is Lee your friend   ☐
5 I'm not Italian   ☐
6 Are they happy   ☐

2 Complete the questions with *Is* or *Are*.

1 *Is* Kit a cat?
2 _____ she black?
3 _____ Kit and Dug friends?
4 _____ they at school?
5 _____ Dug's suit blue and red?
6 _____ his suit too small?

3 Match answers a–f to the questions in Exercise 2.

a ☐ Yes, it is.   d ☐ No, it isn't.
b ☐ Yes, they are.   e ☐ No, they aren't.
c `1` Yes, she is.   f ☐ No, she isn't.

4 Think about Dug and Kit. Complete the answers with your own ideas.

1 Are Dug and Kit cool?
   _____, they _____ .
2 Is he clever?
   _____, he _____ .
3 Is she a good friend?
   _____, she _____ .
4 Is the suit OK?
   _____, it _____ .
5 Are you a superhero?
   _____, I _____ .

5 Complete the dialogue. Use *am/are/is* and the words in brackets.

A: ¹Are you (you) May?
B: Yes, ² _____ .
A: ³ _____ (Ben) your brother?
B: No, ⁴ _____ . He's my classmate.
A: ⁵ _____ (you) best friends?
B: Yes, ⁶ _____ .
A: ⁷ _____ (he) Spanish?
B: Yes, ⁸ _____ . He's from Madrid.

6 Put the words in the correct order to make questions.

1 is What name your ?
   What is your name?
2 at Are school you ?
   _____
3 twelve you Are ?
   _____
4 your best thirteen friend Is ?
   _____
5 best name What friend's is your ?
   _____

7 Answer the questions in Exercise 6 for you.

1 My name _____
2 _____
3 _____
4 _____
5 _____

I can ask for and give personal information.

🔊 04 **Asking for personal information.**
What's your name?
How old are you?
Where are you from?
What's your favourite *music/sport/film*?
Who's your favourite *actor/singer/
sports person*?

1 Complete the dialogue with sentences a–e.

Man: Hi. Welcome to the show. ¹e
Nancy: My name's Nancy.
Man: Where are you from?
Nancy: ² _____
Man: ³ _____
Nancy: I'm twelve.
Man: What's your favourite sport?
Nancy: ⁴ _____
Man: Who's your favourite actor?
Nancy: ⁵ _____

a   Swimming.
b   London, England.
c   Asa Butterfield.
d   How old are you?
e   What's your name?

2 Circle the correct answer.

1   (What)/ Who is your name?
2   What / Where are you from?
3   How / Where old are you?
4   Who / Where is your favourite sports person?
5   What / Who is your favourite film?

3 Match answers a–e to the questions in Exercise 2.

a   ☐ Manchester, England.
b   [1] I'm Danny.
c   ☐ Renato Sanches. He's from Portugal.
d   ☐ *The Incredibles*.
e   ☐ Twelve.

4 Read. Then complete the questions for Emma.

My blog *by* Emma Carter

Hi! I'm Emma and I'm new to Northwood School. I'm ¹twelve, and I'm ²from Cardiff, Wales. My favourite sport is ³tennis, and my favourite book is ⁴*The Hobbit*. My favourite singer is ⁵Alicia Keys.

1   How old *are you*?
2   Where _____ ?
3   What _____ ?
4   What _____ ?
5   Who _____ ?

5 Answer the questions in Exercise 4 for you.

1   I'm _____
2   _____
3   _____
4   _____
5   _____

I can understand a text about a gadget.

OUR CLEVER CLOTHES

1 ☐
Hi, I'm Sam. Look at this – it's a cool jacket, but that's not all. It's an MP3 player too, with my favourite music. My jacket is green and my sister Anna's is red.

A

2 ☐
Hello. I'm Luke. These jeans are my favourite clothes. They're cool and they're clever too. Look. This is a pocket for my mobile phone. It's a phone charger too. My jeans are fantastic!

B

3 ☐
My name's Becky. These trainers are my favourite things. They're red and yellow and they're very cool. Look – what are these? They're small wheels! My trainers are skates too! My trainers are very clever!

C

1 Read the text. Match children 1–3 to their clothes A–C.

2 Read the texts again. Who is it? Choose from the words below. There is one extra name.

> Anna   Becky   Luke   Sam

  1 My favourite things are red and yellow. I'm _____.

  2 I'm Sam's sister. I'm _____.

  3 My favourite clothes are my jeans. I'm _____.

3 **VOCABULARY** Look at the pictures. What can you see? Circle T (true) or F (false).

1 mountain bike   T / F
2 skateboard   T / F
3 laptop computer   T / F
4 games console   T / F

LISTENING and WRITING | Punctuation

I can understand and write short texts about favourite things.

1 Label the pictures with the words below.

> backpack   games console   laptop computer
> mobile phone   mountain bike   ~~trainers~~

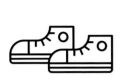

1 ☐ *trainers* 2 ☐ _____

3 ☐ _____ 4 ☐ _____

5 ☐ _____ 6 ☐ _____

2 🔊 05 Listen to Luke and Rosa. What do they talk about? Tick (✓) the pictures in Exercise 1.

3 🔊 05 Listen again. Circle the correct answer.

1 Luke's _____ is new.

a  b

2 Rosa's favourite colour is _____.

a   b

3 Luke's trainers are _____.

a **new**   b **old**

4 Rosa's favourite thing is this _____.

a   b

4 Correct Harry's blog post. Add punctuation marks.

> ,   .   ?   !

Harry's blog

Hi ¹☐
My name is Harry ²☐ My favourite things are my school bag ³☐ my mobile phone and my skateboard ⁴☐ What's my favourite colour ⁵☐ That's easy ⁶☐ It's red ⁷☐

5 Now write a blog post about you. Use punctuation marks.

Hello/Hi! _____

name? _____

_____

favourite things? _____

_____

favourite colour? _____

_____

I can talk and write about different shapes.

1 Look at the shapes and do the puzzle.

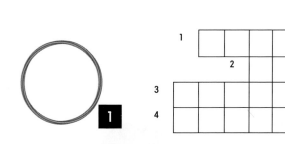

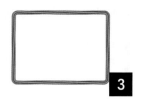

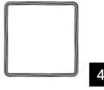

2 Match the people 1–5 to the things a–e.

1 [b]

This is my skirt. It's white with small squares and circles.

2 ☐

These are my new trainers. They're blue with red lines.

3 ☐
This is my new jacket. It's black with small triangles.

4 ☐
This is my school bag. It's blue with big rectangles and small circles.

5 ☐

This is my T-shirt. It's black with white lines and red circles.

3 Look at the things a–e in Exercise 2 again and answer the questions.

1   Look at the jacket.
    What colour are the triangles?   _white_

2   Look at the skirt.
    What colour are the squares?   _____
    What colour are the circles?   _____

3   Look at the T-shirt.
    What colour are the lines?   _____
    What colour are the circles?   _____

4   Look at the trainers.
    What colour are the lines?   _____

5   Look at the school bag.
    What colour are the rectangles?   _____
    What colour are the circles?   _____

4 Look at pictures A and B and count the shapes!

A

B

Picture A
1   circles   _3_
2   squares   _____
3   rectangles   _____
4   lines   _____
5   triangles   _____

Picture B
6   circles   _____
7   squares   _____
8   rectangles   _____
9   lines   _____
10 triangles   _____

SELF-ASSESSMENT

For each learning objective, tick (✓) the box that best matches your ability.

☺☺ = I understand and can help a friend.   ☹ = I understand but have some questions.

☺ = I understand and can do it by myself.   ☹☹ = I do not understand.

		☺☺	☺	☹	☹☹	Need help?	Now try ...
2.1	Vocabulary					Students' Book pp. 24–25 Workbook p. 18	Ex. 1–2, p. 26
2.2	Grammar					Students' Book pp. 26–27 Workbook p. 19	Ex. 5–6, p. 26
2.3	Grammar					Students' Book pp. 28–29 Workbook p. 20	Ex. 7, p. 26
2.4	Communication					Students' Book p. 30 Workbook p. 21	Ex. 8, p. 26
2.5	Reading and Vocabulary					Students' Book p. 31 Workbook p. 22	
2.6	Listening and Writing					Students' Book p. 32 Workbook p. 23	
2.7	CLIL					Students' Book p. 33 Workbook p. 24	

2.1 I can talk about clothes.
2.2 I can use *this*, *that*, *these*, *those* and adjectives.
2.3 I can ask and answer questions with the verb *to be*.
2.4 I can ask for and give personal information.
2.5 I can understand a text about a gadget.
2.6 I can understand and write short texts about favourite things.
2.7 I can talk and write about different shapes.

What can you remember from this unit?

New words I learned (the words you most want to remember from this unit)	**Expressions and phrases I liked** (any expressions or phrases you think sound nice, useful or funny)	**English I heard or read outside class** (e.g. from websites, books, adverts, films, music)

SELF-CHECK

Vocabulary

1 Circle the odd one out.

0	(T-shirt)	trainers	shoes
1	cool	fantastic	boring
2	backpack	top	dress
3	trousers	jeans	cap
4	long	top	big
5	jacket	skirt	coat

/5

2 Look at the photo and write the words.

0 *T-shirt*   3 _____
1 _____   4 _____
2 _____   5 _____

/5

Grammar

3 Circle the correct answer.

0 My shoes _____ too small.
   a is   b (are)
1 _____ T-shirt isn't big.
   a This   b These
2 What _____ it?
   a are   b is
3 _____ are my brothers.
   a That   b Those
4 Jen's trainers _____ cool.
   a are   b is
5 _____ they your books?
   a Is   b Are

/5

4 Answer yes (✓) or no (✗). Use short answers.

0 A: Are you OK?
   B: *Yes, I am.* ✓
1 A: Is it your backpack?
   B: _____ ✓
2 A: Are your new shoes black?
   B: _____ ✗
3 A: Are we friends?
   B: _____ ✓
4 A: Is Tom your brother?
   B: _____ ✗
5 A: Is Ella at school?
   B: _____ ✓

/5

Communication

5 Put the sentences in the dialogue in the correct order.

a ☐ Twelve. Are you twelve too?
b ☐ Harry Potter, book one.
c ☐0 Hello, I'm Benjamin. What's your name?
d ☐ Hi. I'm Jackie. I'm from England. Where are you from?
e ☐ I'm from England too. How old are you?
f ☐ No, I'm not. I'm thirteen. What's your favourite book?

/5

Vocabulary /10
Grammar /10
Communication /5
Your total score /25

Reading and Writing

I am at my birthday party. I have a big cake! I'm thirteen. I'm very happy. The party is at my house. My friends and family are here and my granny and grandad are here too. My grandad isn't British. He's Spanish.

My presents are cool. My favourite present is my new mobile phone. It's blue, my favourite colour. I'm in my new red dress in the photo.

1 Read the text. Complete the sentences with one word in each gap.

0 My *cake* is big.
1 I'm _____ years old.
2 My _____ and family are at the party.
3 My grandad _____ British.
4 My presents _____ cool.
5 My favourite present is my _____ mobile phone.
6 In the photo I'm in my new red_____ .

/6

2 Complete five sentences about Emily. Use *is*, *is from* or *are* and the information in the table.

0	Name	Emily
1	Country	the UK
2	Brother	11
3	Best friend	Katia
4	Favourite colours	blue and white
5	Favourite thing	jacket

0 This *is Emily* .
1 She _____ .
2 Emily's brother _____ .
3 Emily's best friend's name _____ .
4 Emily's favourite colours _____ .
5 Emily's favourite thing _____ .

/6

Listening

3 🔊 06 Listen and tick (✓) the correct answer.

0 Where is Uncle Tom?

 A ☐   B ✓   C ☐

1 What's Lily's favourite birthday present?

 A ☐   B ☐   C ☐

2 What's in the bag?

 A ☐   B ☐   C ☐

3 How old is Jo?

 A ☐   B ☐   C ☐

4 Which is Mrs Smith's dog?

 A ☐   B ☐   C ☐

/4

Communication

4 John is a new student in May's class. Match May's questions 0–4 to John's answers a–f. There is one extra answer.

0 [c] What's your name?
1 ☐ How old are you?
2 ☐ Where are you from?
3 ☐ What's your favourite sport?
4 ☐ Who's your favourite singer?

a It's football.   d British.
b Beyoncé.   e The UK.
c It's John.   f I'm thirteen.

/4

Reading and Writing   /12

Listening   /4

Communication   /4

Your total score   /20

Unit 2 **27**

3

In the house

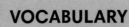

I can talk about my house.

1 Look at the pictures. Circle the correct answer.

1 It's a wall /(a door.)
2 It's an armchair / a desk.
3 It's a floor / a sofa.
4 It's a bed / a chair.

5 It's a desk / a table.
6 It's a fridge / a door.
7 It's a window / a wall.

2 Complete the sentences. Use words from Exercise 1.

1 It's a ___bath___ .   2 It's a _____.   3 It's a _____.

3 Where are these things found? Label the things with the words below.

bathroom   bedroom   garage   garden   ~~kitchen~~   living room

1 _kitchen_   2 _____   3 _____

4 _____   5 _____   6 _____

GRAMMAR   *there is / there are* affirmative; prepositions of place

I can use *there is / there are* and prepositions of place.

1 Circle the correct words. Find the correct picture. Write *A* or *B*.

1 (There is)/ *There are* an armchair.   [B]
2 *There is* / *There are* five chairs.   ☐
3 *There is* / *There are* a small picture.   ☐
4 *There is* / *There are* a bed.   ☐
5 *There is* / *There are* two sofas.   ☐
6 *There is* / *There are* four windows.   ☐

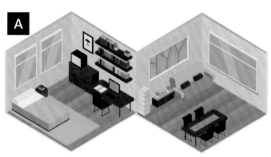

A

B

2 **VOCABULARY** Complete the sentences with the words below.

| in   in   next to   on   on   under |

1 Alex and Lian are *in* the living room.
2 There's a black table _____ the white table.
3 There's a mobile phone _____ the black table.
4 There are trainers _____ the table.
5 There's a chair _____ the living room.
6 There's a school bag _____ the chair.

3 Look and circle the correct answers.

1 *There is* / (are) two girls (in)/ *on* the garden.
2 *There is* / *are* two laptops *under* / *on* the table.
3 *There is* / *are* a bike next *to* / *on* the table.
4 *There is* / *are* two dogs *next to* / *under* the table.
5 *There is* / *are* a cat *on* / *in* the wall.
6 *There is* / *are* a book next *to* / *in* the school bag.

4 Complete the sentences with the words in the box.

| a   are   are   are   in   next   on   there |

1 There ¹*are* blue walls ² _____ my bedroom. There ³ _____ pictures ⁴ _____ the walls.
2 There's ⁵ _____ small table ⁶ _____ to my bed. There ⁷ _____ some books on the table. ⁸ _____ is a laptop too.

5 Write four sentences about your bedroom. Use *in, on, next to, under* and the words below.

| bed   desk   door   window   chair   photos books   box |

1 _____
_____
2 _____
_____
3 _____
_____
4 _____
_____

GRAMMAR   *there is / there are* negative and questions

I can use the negative and question forms of *there is/there are*.

1 Circle the correct answer.

1 There *isn't* /(aren't) any chairs in the kitchen.
2 *Is* / *Are* there any laptops in the classroom?
3 *Is* / *Are* there a cat in the garden?
4 There *isn't* / *aren't* a TV in the living room.
5 *Is* / *Are* there a number on the door?
6 There *isn't* / *aren't* any people in the park.

2 Look at the picture and circle T (true) or F (false).

1 There isn't a table in the living room.   T / (F)
2 There isn't a phone on the table.   T / F
3 There aren't any pictures on the wall.   T / F
4 There isn't a TV in the room.   T / F
5 There aren't two tables in the room.   T / F
6 There aren't any chairs in the room.   T / F

3 Complete the sentences with *There isn't* or *There aren't*.

1 *There isn't* an armchair in the kitchen.
2 _____ any pictures on the wall.
3 _____ a bike in the garage.
4 _____ any sandwiches on the table.
5 _____ a mobile phone on my desk.
6 _____ any books in this bag.

4 Complete the questions with *Is there a* or *Are there any*.

1 *Is there a* laptop in the bedroom?
2 _____ photos on your laptop?
3 _____ cat under the bed?
4 _____ clothes in that bag?
5 _____ bike in the garage?
6 _____ pencils in the bag?

5 Match answers a–f to the questions in Exercise 3.

a ☐ No, there aren't. It's a new laptop.
b ☐ Yes, there are – my new jeans and a T-shirt.
c ☐ Yes, there is. There's a blue mountain bike.
d ☐ No, there aren't. But there are pens and a book.
e [1] Yes, there is. It's on the desk.
f ☐ No, there isn't. But there are two cats on my bed!

6 Write questions. Answer yes (✓) or no (✗). Use short answers.

1 trees / in your garden?
   A: *Are there any trees in your garden?*
   B: *✗ No, there aren't.*
2 a garage / next to your house?
   A: _____
   B: ✗ _____
3 armchairs / in your living room?
   A: _____
   B: ✓ _____ Two armchairs and a sofa.
4 pencils / on your desk?
   A: _____
   B: ✗ _____ They're in my bag!
5 a desk / in your bedroom?
   A: _____
   B: ✓ _____ It's next to the window.

7 Complete the text. Write one word in each gap.

There [1]*are* a lot of things in the garage. There's [2]_____ old fridge and there [3]_____ two old armchairs. Are there [4]_____ bikes? No, there [5]_____ and there isn't [6]_____ car!

I can ask for something and ask where something is.

🔊 **07** Having a guest.

A: Hello. Please, come in.
B: Thank you.
A: Would you like *a sandwich*?
B: Yes, please. / No, thank you.

A: Where's *the bathroom*, please?
B: Let me show you.

---

1 Complete the dialogues.

a It's in the living room. Let me show you.
b Would you like a cake?
c Hi. Come in!
d Where's your laptop?
e Yes, please!
f Thanks.

2 Read the dialogues and circle TWO correct answers.

1 A: Where's the bathroom?
   B: _____
   (a) It's there.
   (b) Let me show you.
   c   Yes, there is.

2 A: Would you like a cake?
   B: _____
   a   No, thanks.
   b   Let me show you.
   c   Yes, please.

3 A: Where's my jacket?
   B: _____
   a   Here it is.
   b   It's on the chair.
   c   Come in.

4 A: Please, come in. Would you like a sandwich?
   B: _____
   a   There's a sandwich.
   b   Yes, please.
   c   No, thanks.

5 A: Where's your bike?
   B: _____
   a   No, it isn't.
   b   In the garden.
   c   At my friend's house.

3 Complete the dialogues. Write one word in each gap.

1 Hello. ¹*Please* come in.

²_____ you.

2 Would you ³_____ a cake?

⁴_____, please.

3 ⁵_____ the bathroom, please?

Let me ⁶_____ you.

A house in a tree!
Luke is on holiday. Look!
His holiday house is in a tree!

This tree house is very cool. There are two bedrooms: one is big and one is small. In the big bedroom there are two beds – for me and my brother. The small bedroom is for my mum and dad.

There's a small kitchen and there's a big living room. There's a table in the kitchen and there are four chairs. In the living room there's a sofa. There isn't a television there.

1 What is there in the tree house? Read and tick (✓).

1 ✓   2 ☐   3 ☐

4 ☐   5 ☐   6 ☐

7 ☐   8 ☐

2 Complete the sentences with one number in each gap.

1 There are _____ rooms in the house.
2 There are _____ big rooms.
3 There are _____ people in Luke's family.

3 Complete the puzzle.

```
        1
         t
2 □□□□   e
    3 □□ l □□
4 □□□□   e
         v
         i
  5 □□□□ s □□
         i
         o
6 □□□□   n
```

LISTENING and WRITING Rooms in a house

I can understand and write short texts about describing a room.

1 🔊 **08 Listen to the dialogue. What's it about? Circle the correct answer.**

a Nancy's new house
b Nancy's bedroom
c Nancy's family

2 🔊 **08 Listen again. Correct the sentences.**

1 In Nancy's house there are five rooms.

_____

2 There are two bedrooms.

_____

3 There's a TV in Nancy's bedroom.

_____

3 🔊 **08 Listen again. Tick (✓) Nancy's house.**

A ☐

B ☐

C ☐

4 Correct Jack's text. Add apostrophes.

MY DREAM BEDROOM

by Jack

In my dream bedroom <u>there's</u> a big bed. Its blue. Next to the bed theres a table with a lamp. On the floor theres a big carpet. Its red, yellow and orange. Theres a computer and there are lots of posters and photos of my friends. There arent any plants in the room and there isnt a TV.

5 Now write about your dream bedroom. Use the ideas below or your own ideas.

| TV computer games console books carpet cushions lamp posters bed desk table sofa fridge |

_____

_____

_____

_____

_____

_____

_____

_____

_____

_____

I can talk and write about different materials.

1 Match the word fragments to make five words and label the pictures.

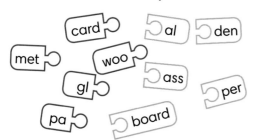

card   al   den
met   woo
gl   ass
per
pa   board

1 _____

2 _____

3 _____

4 _____

5 _____

2 Complete the sentences with the phrases below.

> cardboard house   glass walls   ~~metal monster~~   paper lamp   wooden chair

1 This *metal monster* is my brother's favourite thing!

2 Amy's house is very cool. There are _____ in the house!

3 Look at my cousins, Olivia and Mary! Olivia is in a recycled _____.
It's Olivia and Mary's favourite toy!

4 This _____ is in my granny's living room. It's very, very old and it's from China!

5 This blue and white _____ is next to my bed. It's my favourite thing.

3 Look at the picture. Then complete the sentences with the correct words.

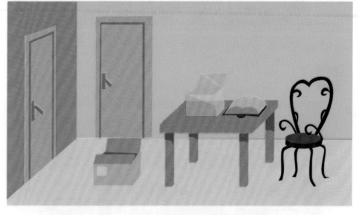

1 The pages of the book aren't glass. They're *p a p e r*!
2 This isn't a cardboard chair. It's a m _ _ _ _ chair!
3 That isn't a wooden box! It's a g _ _ _ _ _ box!
4 This isn't a paper box. It's a c _ _ _ _ _ _ _ _ _ box!
5 Those aren't metal doors. They're w _ _ _ _ _ doors!

For each learning objective, tick (✓) the box that best matches your ability.

☺☺ = I understand and can help a friend.   ☹ = I understand but have some questions.

☺ = I understand and can do it by myself.   ☹☹ = I do not understand.

		☺☺	☺	☹	☹☹	Need help?	Now try ...
1.1	Vocabulary					Students' Book pp. 38–39 Workbook p. 28	Ex. 1–2, p. 36
1.2	Grammar					Students' Book pp. 40–41 Workbook p. 29	Ex. 3, p. 36
1.3	Grammar					Students' Book pp. 42–43 Workbook p. 30	Ex. 4, p. 36
1.4	Communication					Students' Book p. 44 Workbook p. 31	Ex. 5, p. 36
1.5	Reading and Vocabulary					Students' Book p. 45 Workbook p. 32	
1.6	Listening and Writing					Students' Book p. 46 Workbook p. 33	
1.7	CLIL					Students' Book p. 47 Workbook p. 34	

3.1   I can talk about my house.
3.2   I can use *there is / there are* and prepositions of place.
3.3   I can use the negative and question forms of *there is / there are*.
3.4   I can ask for something and ask where something is.
3.5   I can understand a text about a house.
3.6   I can understand and write short texts about rooms in a house.
3.7   I can talk and write about different materials.

What can you remember from this unit?

New words I learned (the words you most want to remember from this unit)	**Expressions and phrases I liked** (any expressions or phrases you think sound nice, useful or funny)	**English I heard or read outside class** (e.g. from websites, books, adverts, films, music)

Vocabulary

1 Look at the pictures and the letters. Label the photos.

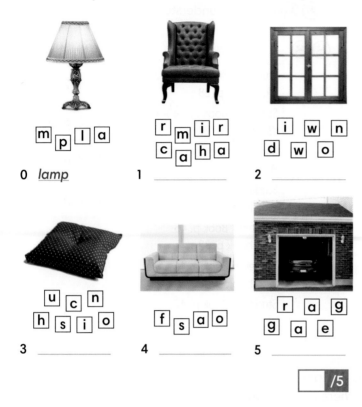

m p l a

0 *lamp*

r m i r
c a h a

1 _____

i w n
d w o

2 _____

u c n
h s i o

3 _____

f s a o

4 _____

r a g
g a e

5 _____

/5

2 Look at the pictures. Circle the correct word.

The mouse is ⁰(*in*)/ *on* the ¹*bathroom* / *bedroom*.
It's ²*under* / *on* the desk.

This is the ³*kitchen* / *living room*. The mouse is ⁴*in* / *next*
to the ⁵*fridge* / *door*.

/5

Grammar

3 Circle the correct answer.

0   There (*isn't*)/ *aren't* a cat in the garden.
1   There *is* / *are* three books on the desk.
2   There isn't *a pen* / *any pens* in my bag.
3   There *isn't* / *aren't* any chairs in the classroom.
4   There *is* / *are* a book on the desk.
5   There *are* / *aren't* any plants in the living room.

/5

4 Complete the dialogues with one word in each gap.

1   A: ⁰*Is* there a television in the kitchen?
    B: No, there ¹_____ .
2   A: ²_____ there ³_____ posters on the wall?
    B: No, there ⁴_____ .
3   A: Is there ⁵_____ computer in your bedroom?
    B: Yes, there is.

/5

Communication

5 Put the sentences in the dialogue in the correct order.

a ☐ It's in the living room. Let me show you.
b ☐ No, thank you. Where's your new television?
c ☐ Oh wow! Cool!
d 0 Hi! Please come in.
e ☐ Thanks.
f ☐ Would you like a drink?

/5

Vocabulary   /10
Grammar   /10
Communication   /5
Your total score /25

1 Look at the pictures and complete the sentences with the words below.

cottage   ~~detached~~   flats   houseboat   semi-detached   terraced

1   This is a *detached* house.

4   This is a _____ .

2   These are _____ houses.

5   These are _____ houses.

3   This is a _____ .

6   This is a block of _____ .

2 Match 1–4 to a–d.

1   ☐
That's my house! It's small and the garden is small too. My house is in the country. There aren't lots of people here but there are lots of trees and flowers.

2   ☐
My house is in a big city. My friend Jason's house is next to my house. And my friend Lisa's house is next to my house too!

3   ☐
My home isn't in the city. There aren't a lot of rooms and the rooms are very small. There isn't a garden but there's a lot of water!

4   ☐
My home is in the city. There isn't a garden, but the view from my bedroom window is fantastic! There are a lot of people in this block.

a   My home is a terraced house.
b   My home is a flat.

c   My home is a cottage.
d   My home is a houseboat.

4

About me

I can describe someone's face and hair.

1 Write words 1–5 describing the face.

1	*ear*	3	_____	5	_____
2	_____	4	_____		

2 Look at the pictures. Circle the correct answers.

1 (short) / long   2 straight / spiky   3 curly / wavy   4 short / long
(blond) / red   red / brown   black / blond   dark / blond

3 Look and complete the sentences.

1 Jake's hair is s _h o r_ t and s _ _ _ _ .

2 Lin's hair is l _ _ _ and s _ _ _ _ _ _ _ .

3 Diego's hair is c _ _ _ _ _ and b _ _ _ _ .

4 Martha's hair is w _ _ _ and b _ _ _ _ .

4 Look and complete the sentences with the words In the box.

> big ~~black~~ blond brown green grey ~~long~~
> long short ~~small~~ small straight

1 *long* wavy *black* hair and *small* blue eyes
2 short _____ brown hair and big _____ eyes
3 _____ curly _____ hair and _____ eyes
4 _____ straight _____ hair and _____ blue eyes

5 Do these words describe eyes or hair? Write E (eyes) or H (hair).

1	wavy	*H*	3 blond	☐	5 short	☐
2	big	☐	4 straight	☐	6 small	☐

I can use the affirmative and negative forms of *have got*.

1 Circle the correct word.

1 I (have) / *has* got two brothers.
2 My granny *have* / *has* got curly white hair.
3 We *have* / *has* got a small car.
4 The students *have* / *has* got a very good teacher.
5 Ben *have* / *has* got big feet.
6 You *have* / *has* got very long hair.
7 My cat *have* / *has* got yellow eyes.
8 I *have* / *has* got brown eyes and brown hair.

2 Write affirmative (✓) and negative (✗) sentences.

1 Alex / a new mobile phone ✓
   Alex has got a new mobile phone.
2 He / a new skateboard ✗
   _____
3 Jen / a new coat ✗
   _____
4 She / a new skirt ✓
   _____
5 Alex and Jenny / a cat ✗
   _____
6 They / a games console ✓
   _____

3 Match 1–4 to parts of the body. Use the words below.

| arm feet fingers hand ~~head~~ |

1 *head*   2 _____

3 _____   4 _____ and _____

4 Complete the texts with plural nouns. Then match the texts to the photos.

A

a snake

B

a crocodile

1 ☐ I've got four short ¹**leg**s (leg). My ² _____ (foot) are small. I've got two ³ _____ (eye) and a big head.
2 ☐ I've got a long body. I haven't got any ⁴ _____ (leg) or ⁵ _____ (foot). I've got two ⁶ _____ (eye). I haven't got any ⁷ _____ (ear).

5 Complete the text with affirmative (✓) and negative (✗) forms of the verb *have got*.

Hi! My name is Ben. I'm twelve. I ¹**'ve got** (✓) two sisters. I ² _____ (✗) any brothers.
We ³ _____ (✓) two pets – a rabbit and a cat. The cat's name is Softy but the rabbit ⁴ _____ (✗) a name.
My school is big. We ⁵ _____ (✓) lots of teachers. I'm in class 7. My best friend's name is Zack. He ⁶ _____ (✓) curly brown hair and big ears!

I can ask questions with *have got* and use *his, her, its, our, your, their.*

1 Circle the correct answer.

1 (Have) / *Has* X1 and X2 got big heads?
2 *Have / Has* I got super powers?
3 *Have / Has* Dug got a good friend?
4 *Have / Has* you got super ears?
5 *Have / Has* Kit got green eyes?
6 *Have / Has* Dug and Kit got super eyes?

2 Match answers a–d to the questions in Exercise 1.

a ☐ No, I haven't.
b ☐ No, you haven't.
c ☐ Yes, he has.
d ☐ 1 Yes, they have.
e ☐ No, they haven't
f ☐ Yes, she has.

3 Make questions with *have got.*

1 *Have* we *got* super powers?
2 _____ your classmates _____ super powers?
3 _____ your brother _____ a lot of friends?
4 _____ you _____ a sister?
5 _____ your Granny _____ a computer?
6 _____ your parents _____ a new car?

4 Write true short answers for the questions in Exercise 3.

1 *No, we haven't.*
2 _____
3 _____
4 _____
5 _____
6 _____

5 Look and complete with *His, Her, Its, Our, Your* or *Their.*

1 My brothers are young. *Their* bikes aren't fast.

2 This cat is small. _____ legs are short.

3 Grandad's got grey hair. _____ eyes are brown.

4 Well done, Anna and Lily! _____ homework is very good.

5 We've got a car. _____ car is big!

6 Julie's clothes are black and white. _____ skateboard is blue.

6 Look and complete the dialogues with the words below.

| any got ~~Has~~ Have haven't His its Their 've |

A: ¹*Has* Jimmy ²_____ a dog?
B: Yes, he has. ³_____ dog has got short legs, but ⁴_____ ears are very long.

A: ⁵_____ you got ⁶_____ sisters?
B: Yes, I ⁷_____ got two sisters. ⁸_____ names are Lea and Anika. But I ⁹_____ got any brothers.

COMMUNICATION · Apologies

I can say sorry and respond to an apology.

🔊 09 **Apologising.**

A: I'm so sorry.	B: It's OK.
Sorry about that!	That's all right.
Sorry, my mistake.	No problem.

1 Put the sentences in the dialogues in the correct order.

1 a ☐ Are you sure?
  b ☐ It's OK.
  c [1] Oh no! I'm so sorry!
  d ☐ Yes, it's all right.

2 a ☐ Oh, my mistake. Here you are.
  b ☐ Thanks.
  c ☐ Hey! That's my book!

3 a ☐ That's all right.
  b ☐ Yes, no problem.
  c ☐ Oops! Sorry!
  d ☐ Are you sure?

2 Read the dialogues. Circle the correct answer.

1 A: I'm sorry.
  B: ⓐ That's all right.
    b Thank you.

2 A: Sorry about that!
  B: a No problem.
    b Are you sure?

3 A: Oh no! Look at that! I'm so sorry!
  B: a Yes, 'I'm fine.
    b It's OK.

4 A: Sorry, it's my mistake.
  B: a Are you sure?
    b That's all right.

5 A: Where's my book?
  B: a Sorry, my mistake.
    b Sorry, I've got it.

3 Complete the dialogues with one word in each gap.

1 A: I can't find my book!
  B: I've got it! ¹**Sorry** about that.
  A: ² _____ all right.

2 A: Oops! I'm so ³ _____ !
  B: It's OK.
  A: Are you ⁴ _____ ?
  B: Yes, no ⁵ _____ .

3 A: These aren't my keys.
  B: Sorry, my ⁶ _____ . Here you are.
  C: It's ⁷ _____ .

4 Look at the picture. Complete the dialogue.

Matt: *Jason, that's my bag!*

Jason: _____

Matt: _____

I can understand a text about personalities.

Hi. My name's Tim. I'm twelve and I'm from London. I've got two brothers, three sisters and ... ten cousins!

I've got a lot of books, a bike and a skateboard. I'm not good at sports but my best friend is very good at football. His name is Max.

Max is my neighbour too. Our favourite place is his garden. We've got a little house in a tree! Max has got a sister. Her name is Lucy and she's very clever. Max and I aren't good at Maths, but Lucy is helpful! She's very nice!

1 Read the text. What is it about? Tick (✓) the correct pictures.

1 ✓

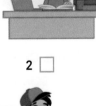

2 ☐

3 ☐

4 ☐

5 ☐

6 ☐

2 Read the text again. Circle T (true) or F (false).

1 Tim's got a big family.   Ⓣ/ F
2 There are two boys in Tim's family. T / F
3 Tim has got a lot of books.   T / F
4 Max has got a garden.   T / F
5 Lucy is Tim's sister.   T / F

3 Complete the sentences with the words below.

| clever   friendly   funny   ~~helpful~~

This is Rose. She's my cousin. She's ¹*helpful*.

This is Damian. He's my cousin. He's very ² _____.

This is my friend Paul. He's ³ _____.

Sylvia is my sister. She's ⁴ _____.

LISTENING and WRITING   Animals

I can understand and write a short text about an animal.

1 🔊 **10 Listen and put the photos in the correct order. Write 1–3.**

a panda ☐

a dolphin ☐

an ostrich ☐

2 🔊 **10 Listen again. Tick (✓) for yes and put a cross (✗) for no.**

	dolphins	pandas	ostriches
friendly	✓		
funny			
clever			

3 Read the text. Divide it into two paragraphs.

Elephants are very big! They've got big bodies, big ears and very long trunks. Elephants aren't very friendly. Sometimes they're helpful. They're clever, too.

4 Circle the correct answer.

Paragraph 1 / Paragraph 2 is about elephants' personalities.

5 Write two paragraphs about tigers. Use the words in the box and your own ideas.

Tigers
Paragraph 1
big
yellow eyes
yellow, black and white
Paragraph 2
clever (✓)
friendly (✗)

Tigers

_____
_____
_____
_____
_____
_____
_____
_____
_____
_____
_____
_____
_____
_____
_____
_____

I can talk and write about genes.

1 Look at the pictures and do the puzzle. What is the mystery word?

1 He's _____ 2 He's _____ 3 They're _____ 4 They're the _____

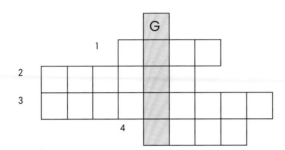

Mystery word: _____

2 Colour in Fizzy, Filly and Fleeb's hair and eyes.

B	blue – strong
Y	yellow – strong
g	green – weak
r	red – weak

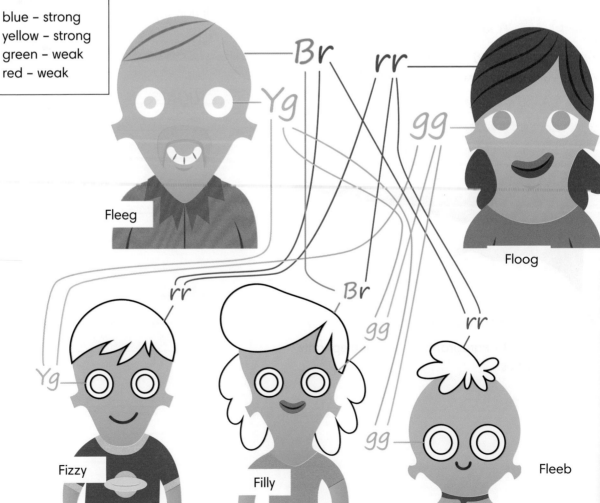

SELF-ASSESSMENT

For each learning objective, tick (✓) the box that best matches your ability.

☺☺ = I understand and can help a friend.   ☹ = I understand but have some questions.

☺ = I understand and can do it by myself.   ☹☹ = I do not understand.

		☺☺	☺	☹	☹☹	Need help?	Now try ...
4.1	Vocabulary					Students' Book pp. 52–53 Workbook p. 38	Ex. 1–2, p. 46
4.2	Grammar					Students' Book pp. 54–55 Workbook p. 39	Ex. 3, p. 46
4.3	Grammar					Students' Book pp. 56–57 Workbook p. 40	Ex. 4, p. 46
4.4	Communication					Students' Book p. 58 Workbook p. 41	Ex. 5, p. 46
4.5	Reading and Vocabulary					Students' Book p. 59 Workbook p. 42	
4.6	Listening and Writing					Students' Book p. 60 Workbook p. 43	
4.7	CLIL					Students' Book p. 61 Workbook p. 44	

4.1   I can describe someone's face and hair.
4.2   I can use the affirmative and negative forms of *have got*.
4.3   I can ask questions with *have got* and use *his, her, its, our, your, their*.
4.4   I can say sorry and respond to an apology.
4.5   I can understand and do a personality quiz.
4.6   I can understand and write a short text about animals.
4.7   I can talk and write about genes.

What can you remember from this unit?

New words I learned (the words you most want to remember from this unit)	Expressions and phrases I liked (any expressions or phrases you think sound nice, useful or funny)	English I heard or read outside class (e.g. from websites, books, adverts, films, music)

Vocabulary

1 Match the words to the categories.

| big | ~~blond~~ helpful legs nose wavy |

Hair: 0 *blond*, 1 _____
Eyes: 2 _____
Face: 3 _____
Body: 4 _____
Personality: 5 _____

/5

2 Look at the pictures. Complete the expressions with the words below.

| clever curly friendly ~~funny~~ long straight |

0 very *funny* hair

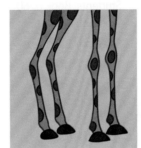

1 very _____ legs

2 _____ hair

3 _____ red hair

4 nice and _____

5 very _____

/5

Grammar

3 Complete the dialogues with *have*, *haven't*, *has*, *hasn't* or *got*.

1 A: Mark ^{0}*has* got brown eyes.
   ^{1}_____ he got brown hair too?
   B: No. His hair is black. His parents and all his brothers have ^{2}_____ black hair.
2 A: ^{3}_____ you got a new bike?
   B: No, I ^{4}_____. It's my old bike.
3 Ann ^{5}_____ got any sisters, but she's got one brother.

/5

4 Complete the sentences with *his*, *her*, *its*, *your*, *our* or *their*.

0 Hello. What are **your** names, please?
1 I've got two cousins. _____ names are Clare and Joe.
2 Grandad's hair is grey and _____ eyes are blue.
3 I've got one sister. _____ name is Paula.
4 We're best friends. _____ names are Katie and Dee.
5 That dog is big and _____ ears are very long!

/5

Communication

5 Complete the dialogues with the words and phrases below.

| all right It's mistake problem ~~so sorry~~ sure |

A: Hello, Danny.
B: My name isn't Danny. It's Tom.
A: Oh, I'm ^{0}**so sorry**!
B: No ^{1}_____!
A: Hey! You've got my bag!
B: Oops! My ^{2}_____! Sorry.
A: That's ^{3}_____.

A: Ouch! Your bag is on my foot!
B: Sorry!
A: ^{4}_____ OK.
A: Are you ^{5}_____?

/5

Vocabulary /10
Grammar /10
Communication /5
Your total score /25

Reading and Writing

Patty's blog **My new band!**

I'm in a band with Jake and Mick from my class. In the photo, they're in my garage!

Jake and Mick are very nice. Jake's twelve. He's got short dark hair and big brown eyes. He's tall. He's good at the guitar because he's got big hands and long fingers. Mick's thirteen. He's got blond wavy hair and small brown eyes. He's short. He's good at the guitar too. I've got a guitar but I'm the singer in our band.

Bye!

1 Read the text. Circle T (True) or F (False).

0	There are four children in the band.	T / (F)
1	Jake is short.	T / F
2	Jake hasn't got blond hair.	T / F
3	Mick's got wavy hair and big brown eyes.	T / F
4	Mick is good at the guitar.	T / F
5	Patty hasn't got a guitar.	T / F

[ ] /5

2 Complete the text with the words below.

> are ~~house~~ got kitchen next to our
> sister small

We've got a new ⁰**house**! There ¹_____ two bedrooms. One bedroom is for my parents and one bedroom is for me and my ²_____. In ³_____ bedroom we've got two beds, two desks and two chairs. There's a living room, a ⁴_____ and a bathroom. There's a ⁵_____ garden and there's a garage too.

We've ⁶_____ a lot of things in the garage! There's an old bed ⁷_____ one wall. My new house is cool.

[ ] /7

Listening

3 🔊 11 Listen and circle the correct words.

0 Anne has got a (computer game)/ skateboard.

1 Charlie's computer is in *his bedroom* / *the kitchen*.

2 Charlie's dad is in the *garden* / *garage*.

3 Charlie's brother has got short *curly* / *spiky* blonde hair.

4 There's a *cat* / *box* under the table.

Communication

4 The Smith family are at granny and grandad's new house. Match pictures 0–4 to sentences a–e.

a	Let me show you.	d	Please come in.
b	Would you like an ice cream?	e	Look! There's a big garden!
c	I'm so sorry!		

Reading and Writing [ ] /4

[ ] /12

Listening [ ] /4

Communication [ ] /4

Your total score [ ] /20

Unit 4 **47**

5

Things I can do

I can understand and use action verbs.

1 Look at the picture. Match a–h to 1–8.

1	e jump	4	☐ ride	7	☐ swim
2	☐ draw	5	☐ run	8	☐ read
3	☐ fly	6	☐ dance		

2 Cross out two letters to find action verbs.

a͟ f i d͟ x	a e c t m	i s i r n g
1 *fix*	2 _____	3 _____

c o r o a k	w o r i t d e
4 _____	5 _____

3 Complete the sentences with the words below.

Cook   Fix   Fly   ~~Read~~   Ride   Write

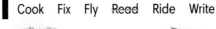

1 *Read* the book.   2 _____ the kite.   3 _____ this, please.

4 _____ those.   5 _____ your name, please.   6 _____ your bike.

I can use the verb *can* in affirmative and negative sentences.

1 Circle the correct answer.

1 The girl (can) / can't read.
2 The man can / can't cook.
3 The cat can / can't write.

4 She can / can't run.
5 He can / can't fix a bike.
6 The bird can / can't fly.

2 Complete the sentences with can (✓) or can't (✗).

1 I _can_ sing well. ✓
2 Sue _____ run fast. ✗
3 Grandad _____ play computer games. ✗
4 My mum _____ skateboard. ✓
5 Dad _____ cook very well. ✗
6 You _____ draw very good pictures. ✓
7 My sister _____ sing and dance. ✓
8 I _____ fix my bike. ✗

3 Write sentences with can or can't.

1 Lian / draw animals ✓
Lian _can draw animals._

2 Lucas / sing well ✗
Lucas _____.

3 Alex / fix computers ✓
Alex _____.

4 Granny / play the guitar ✗
Granny _____.

5 Jen / make cakes ✓
Jen _____.

4 Are sentences 1–6 true? Answer yes (✓) or no (✗). Correct the false sentences.

1 Cats can't climb trees. ☒ _Cats can climb trees._
2 Dogs can't jump. ☐ _____
3 I can fly. ☐ _____
4 Dogs can read. ☐ _____
5 My best friend can't cook. ☐ _____
6 I can't read Chinese. ☐ _____

5 Complete with *play*, *make* or *ride*. What about you? Tick (✓) for yes.

1 _play_ football ☐
2 _____ a poster ☐
3 _____ a horse ☐
4 _____ a bike ☐
5 _____ the piano ☐
6 _____ cakes ☐

6 Complete with *can* or *can't* and the words below to make sentences that are true for you.

| ~~draw~~ fix make play run ride |

1 I _can draw_ pictures.
2 I _____ the guitar.
3 I _____ cakes.
4 I _____ computers.
5 I _____ a horse.
6 I _____ fast.

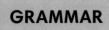

I can ask and answer questions with the verb *can*.

1 Read the sentences and write questions.

1 They can swim.   *Can they swim?*
2 I can draw.   _____
3 Tom can run fast.   _____
4 May can sing well.   _____
5 We can help.   _____
6 The horse can jump.   _____

2 Look at the picture. Answer the questions with the short answers below.

> Yes, he can.   No, he can't.   No, she can't.
> No, it can't.   ~~Yes, they can.~~   No, they can't.

1 Can Kit and Dug see the
    boat?   *Yes, they can.*
2 Can the boy and girl swim?   _____
3 Can their mum swim?   _____
4 Can Dug swim?   _____
5 Can the small dog help?   _____
6 Can Dug help?   _____

3 Write questions.

1 you / fix a bike?
   Can you fix a bike?
2 you / play football?
   _____
3 your mum / cook well?
   _____
4 your classmates / sing?
   _____
5 you / ride a horse?
   _____
6 your best friend / play the piano?
   _____

4 Answer the questions in Exercise 3 so that they are true for you.

1 _____
2 _____
3 _____
4 _____
5 _____
6 _____

5 Complete the dialogues with the correct form of the verb *can* and the verbs below.

> dance   help   play   see

1 A: [1]*Can* you [2]_____ those red apples?
   B: Yes, I [3]_____
   A: [4]_____ you [5]_____ me, please? I'm
     too short.
   B: No problem.

2 A: [6]_____ they [7]_____?
   B: Yes, they [8]_____.
   A: [9]_____ the girl [10]_____ the piano too?
   B: No, she [11]_____.

I can make suggestions about what to do.

🔊 **12 Suggestions**

A: Let's do something fun!
Let's go ice skating!
We can go to the park!

B: 🙂 I agree!
Let's do that!
Great idea!
🙂 I'm not sure.
☹ It's not a good idea.

---

1 Match 1–6 to a–f.

1 [e] Let's play   a the park.
2 [ ] We can swim   b for your birthday.
3 [ ] Let's have a   c chocolate cakes.
     party   d our bikes.
4 [ ] Let's ride   e football after
5 [ ] We can go to   school.
6 [ ] Let's make   f in the swimming
                        pool.

---

2 Complete the expressions and draw a face.

1 Let's do _t h a t_! 🙂
2 It's not a _ _ _ _ _ idea. 🙂
3 Great _ _ _ _ _! 🙂
4 I'm not _ _ _ _ _. 🙂
5 I _ _ _ _ _ _ _! 🙂

---

3 Complete the dialogue with the words below.

| can   haven't   idea   ~~Let's~~   play   sure

A: Hi! [1]**Let's** play in the garden.
B: No, not the garden again. We
   [2]_____ go to the park.
A: Yes, great [3]_____! We can
   [4]_____ football.
B: I'm not [5]_____.
A: Why not?
B: We [6]_____ got a ball.

---

4 Circle the correct answer.

1 A: Let's watch TV.
   B: Yes, I _____.
     (a) agree   b 'm sure
2 A: Let's _____ to the park.
   B: OK.
     a go   b can go
3 A: We can play a computer game.
   B: _____
     a Yes, I can.   b Great idea.
4 A: Let's go to the park.
   B: _____
     a I'm sure.   b That's not a good
                         idea.
5 A: We _____ make sandwiches.
   B: Let's do that.
     a can   b can't

---

5 Write the suggestions and replies.

1 A: play a game
   B: 🙂
   A: _We can play_
      a game!
   B: _____

2 A: make
     sandwiches
   B: 🙂
   A: _____
   B: _____

3 A: go there
   B: ☹
   A: _____
   B: _____

I can understand a text about a hearing dog.

This is twelve-year-old Jasmine. She's with her best friend. Her best friend can't speak to Jasmine. He can't speak any languages! He isn't a boy and he isn't a girl. He's a special dog and his name is Henry.

Jasmine can't hear. She can't hear her friends, she can't hear music and she can't hear cars. But Jasmine is OK. She's got Henry, and Henry is her ears! Henry is a special 'hearing dog' and he can help Jasmine a lot! He can help her walk to school and the park too.

1 Read the text and choose the best title. Circle the correct answer.

a   A dog helps a girl
b   A girl helps her dog
c   Henry has got a problem

2 Read the text again. Circle the correct answer.

1   Jasmine is *eleven* / (*twelve*) years old.
2   Jasmine's best friend *is* / *isn't* a boy.
3   *Henry* / *Jasmine* is a special dog.
4   Jasmine has got *lots of friends* / *one friend*.
5   Jasmine *can* / *can't* hear cars.

3 Read the text again. Match 1–5 to a–e.

1   [c]   Henry is Jasmine's
2   [ ]   Henry can
3   [ ]   Jasmine's best friend
4   [ ]   Jasmine can't
5   [ ]   Jasmine can

a   help Jasmine.
b   hear her friends.
c   ears.
d   is a dog.
e   go to the park with Henry.

4 Look at the pictures and complete the sentences.

see

1   You can see people with your e __ __ s.

hear

2   You can hear music with your e __ __ s.

smell

3   You can smell people with your n __ __ e.

5 Complete the dialogue with the words below.

| ~~hear~~   learn   sign language   speak   special |

A: Look at these women. They can't ¹*hear*.
B: Can they ²_____ English?
A: No, they can't, but they can speak a ³_____ language.
B: Can I ⁴_____ this language?
A: Yes, you can. I can teach you. It's ⁵_____ and you make words with your hands.

I can understand and write short texts about after-school clubs.

1   **What's this? Write the letters in the correct order.**

e	d	a	t	y	r	e	b	d
1	2	3	4	5	6	7	8	9

4	1	9	2	5

8	7	3	6

2   🔊 13   **Listen and circle the correct answer.**

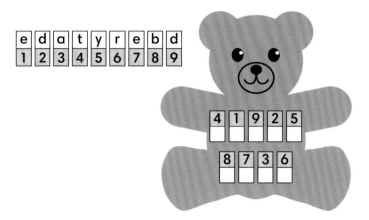

At this club you can *make a new teddy bear / fix an old teddy bear.*

3   🔊 13   **Listen again. Which is the correct teddy bear? Tick (✓).**

A ☐   B ☐   C ☐

4   🔊 13   **Listen again. Circle the correct answer.**

1   What is the girl's name?
    Her name is *Sarah / Erin.*

2   Is the teddy bear Tommy's or his sister's?
    It's *Tommy's / his sister's.*

3   Can Sarah fix it?
    Yes, she can. / No, she can't.

4   What colour are the new eyes?
    They're black. / They're blue.

5   **Complete the blog post with *and* or *but*.**

Come to our new **Fix It Club**! It's fun [1]*and* it's free!
We can fix clothes [2]_____ bikes. We can fix computers [3]_____ we can't fix cars. Sorry! You can watch us [4]_____ you can learn to fix things too. We are at the Youth Club every Saturday morning, [5]_____ not in the afternoon.

Come and visit us soon!

6   **Write a blog post about the basketball club. Use these notes.**

BASKETBALL CLUB
learn to play • watch great games • make friends • have fun • in the School Hall • every Sunday • not in school holidays

Come to our new BASKETBALL CLUB

_____
_____
_____
_____
_____
_____
_____
_____
_____
_____
_____
_____
_____

I can talk and write about musical instruments.

1 Look at the pictures and do the puzzle.

Across

 1

 4

 3

4

 5

6

Down

2

2 Read and write the instruments.

1 This instrument has got a very big brown or black body. You play the black and white keys with your fingers.	*piano*
2 These instruments are electric.	
3 This instrument is Spanish.	
4 This instrument isn't very big. You play the black and white keys with your fingers.	
5 These instruments have got a body and a neck.	
6 This wooden instrument is small.	
7 When you play this instrument, its body is on your legs.	
8 You play this with your feet and your hands.	

3 What instruments can the people play?
Do the puzzle and find the answers.

1 Alice can play the _drums_ .
  C2 + B2 + D5
2 Martin can play the _____.
  A3 + D4
3 Becky can play the _____.
  A4 + D2 + B3 + D1 + C1 + B4 + C5
4 Richard can play the _____.
  B1 + C4 + A1 + B5 + D3
5 Millie can play the _____.
  B5 + A5 + A2 + C3 + C1 + B4 + C5

	A	B	C	D
1	BO	K	GU	IC
2	S	U	DR	ECT
3	VIO	R	TIC	RD
4	EL	I	EY	LIN
5	COU	A	TAR	MS

SELF-ASSESSMENT

For each learning objective, tick (✓) the box that best matches your ability.

😊😊 = I understand and can help a friend.

😊 = I understand and can do it by myself.

☹ = I understand but have some questions.

☹☹ = I do not understand.

		😊😊	😊	☹	☹☹	Need help?	Now try ...
1.1	Vocabulary					Students' Book pp. 66–67 Workbook p. 48	Ex. 1–2, p. 56
1.2	Grammar					Students' Book pp. 68–69 Workbook p. 49	Ex. 3, p. 56
1.3	Grammar					Students' Book pp. 70–71 Workbook p. 50	Ex. 4, p. 56
1.4	Communication					Students' Book p. 72 Workbook p. 51	Ex. 5, p. 56
1.5	Reading and Vocabulary					Students' Book p. 73 Workbook p. 52	
1.6	Listening and Writing					Students' Book p. 74 Workbook p. 53	
1.7	CLIL					Students' Book p. 75 Workbook p. 54	

5.1   I can understand action verbs.

5.2   I can use the verb *can* in affirmative and negative sentences.

5.3   I can ask and answer questions with the verb *can*.

5.4   I can make suggestions about what to do.

5.5   I can understand a text about a hearing dog.

5.6   I can understand and write short texts about after-school clubs.

5.7   I can talk and write about musical instruments.

What can you remember from this unit?

New words I learned (the words you most want to remember from this unit)	**Expressions and phrases I liked** (any expressions or phrases you think sound nice, useful or funny)	**English I heard or read outside class** (e.g. from websites, books, adverts, films, music)

Vocabulary

1 What can they do? Write the action verbs.

0 *fly*

1 _____

2 _____

3 _____

4 _____

5 _____

/5

2 Circle the correct word.

0 (draw) / read a picture
1 play / ride the guitar
2 play / make a cake
3 sing / read a book
4 ride / act a bike
5 sing / play computer games

/5

Grammar

3 Look at the table. Complete the sentences with *can, can't, and* or *but*.

	swim	run fast	fix a bike
Anna	✓	✓	✗
Tom	✗	✓	✓
Sam and Joe	✓	✓	✗

Anna can swim ⁰*and* she ⁰⁰*can* run fast.
Tom ¹_____ run fast ²_____ he can fix a bike.
Sam and Joe can swim ³_____ they ⁴_____ fix a bike.
Tom and Anna ⁵_____ run fast.

/5

4 Look at the picture. Write questions. Answer yes (✓) or no (✗). Use short answers.

1 she / play the piano?
  A: ⁰*Can she play the piano?*
  B: ✓ ¹_____
2 the dogs / sing
  A: ² _____
  B: ✗ ³_____
3 the boy / ride his bike
  A: ⁴ _____
  B: ✓ ⁵_____

/5

Communication

5 Complete the dialogue with one word in each gap.

Amy: ⁰*Let's* do something.
Jack: OK. We ¹_____ make a chocolate cake!
Amy: I'm not ²_____. I ³_____ cook very well.
Jack: No ⁴_____. I can teach you.
Amy: OK, cool. ⁵_____ idea!

/5

Vocabulary   /10
Grammar   /10
Communication   /5
Your total score   /25

1 Look at the pictures and complete the names.

| Eye   Park   Museum   Thames

1   the _____

2   Hyde _____

3   the Natural History _____

4   the London _____

2 Match the word fragments to make six words. Label the pictures.

skate   bo   pic   dino   at   tist   nic   pup   scien   board   pet   saur

1   _____

2   _____

3   _____

4   _____

5   _____

6   _____

3 Match sentences 1–8 to the places a–e. You can use the places a–e more than once.

1   It's next to the Thames.   *b*
2   You can be a scientist for a day there.   ☐
3   You can draw funny people there.   ☐
4   You can make your own comic book there.   ☐
5   You can play football and skateboard there. ☐
6   You can see dinosaurs there.   ☐
7   You can see London from the top.   ☐
8   You can see London from a boat from there.   ☐

a   the Thames
b   the London Eye
c   Hyde Park
d   the Natural History Museum
e   the Cartoon Museum

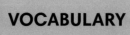

6

My day

I can talk about daily activities.

1 What can you do in these rooms? Tick (✓) for yes and put a cross (✗) for no.

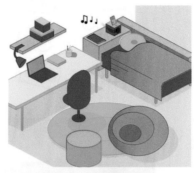

1 ✓ tidy my room
   ☐ have a shower
   ☐ listen to music
   ☐ do my homework
   ☐ hang out with my friends

2 ☐ have lessons
   ☐ have lunch
   ☐ watch TV
   ☐ get up
   ☐ have breakfast

2 Find and circle eight words. Then complete the expressions.

F	D	R	R	E	W	O	R	Y	T	C	S
R	I	H	O	M	E	W	O	R	K	A	H
I	N	O	L	U	Y	F	O	P	P	O	O
E	N	T	V	S	G	E	M	X	I	W	W
N	E	E	Q	I	E	C	K	D	S	S	E
D	R	R	S	C	H	O	O	L	O	M	R

1 do my *homework*
2 tidy my _____
3 have _____
4 have a _____

5 listen to _____
6 go to _____
7 watch _____
8 hang out with my _____

3 Complete the sentences with the words below.

| do get up go go
| ~~have~~ have

1 I *have* lessons.
2 I _____ in the morning.
3 I _____ my homework.
4 I _____ to bed.
5 I _____ to school.
6 I _____ breakfast.

4 Write the sentences in Exercise 3 in the order you do them on a typical day.

6 _____
5 _____
4 *I have lessons.*
3 _____
2 _____
1 _____

I can use the Present Simple in affirmative sentences.

1 Circle the correct answer.

1 Jen *watch* / (*watches*) TV after dinner.
2 Alex *do* / *does* his homework in his room.
3 Lucas and Alex *play* / *plays* football in the park.
4 Jen and Alex *get* / *gets* up late.
5 Lucas's mum *listen* / *listens* to music in the kitchen.
6 Lucas *go* / *goes* to school with Jen and Alex.

2 Complete the table.

I/you/we/they	he/she/it
play	¹*plays*
² _____	does
draw	³ _____
⁴ _____	drinks
⁵ _____	looks
wash	⁶ _____
carry	⁷ _____
⁸ _____	makes

3 Write sentences about Sam.

1 I have breakfast at seven o'clock.

Sam has breakfast at seven o'clock.

2 I go to school with my sister.

_____

3 I do my homework before dinner.

_____

4 I watch TV after dinner.

_____

5 I play football with my friends.

_____

6 I tidy my bedroom every weekend.

_____

7 I visit my grandparents.

_____

4 Complete the sentences. Put the verbs in the correct form.

1 My brother and I *like* (like) orange juice but my sister _____ (drink) milk.

2 Mum and dad _____ (watch) TV and my sister and I _____ (play) computer games after dinner.

3 Rob _____ (tidy) his room and he _____ (help) in the kitchen too.

4 Sue _____ (have) sandwiches for lunch. She _____ (eat) them in the classroom.

5 I _____ (hang out) with my friends after school. Then I _____ (have) dinner.

6 Harry _____ (do) his homework and then he _____ (watch) TV.

5 Complete the table. Write sentences that are true for you.

	Laura	Me
1 has lunch		_____
2 do homework		_____
3 play		_____
4 like		_____

1 Laura *has lunch at school*.

I _____ at _____.

2 Laura _____ her _____.

I _____ my _____.

3 Laura _____.

I _____.

4 Laura _____.

I _____.

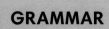

I can use adverbs of frequency.

1 Complete the sentences with adverbs of frequency.

1   Jack ■□□□ _sometimes_ cycles to school

2   Emma ■■■■ _____ has breakfast at home

3   Pete ■■■□ _____ does his homework in his bedroom.

4   I ■□□□ _____ play in the park.

5   We □□□□ _____ watch TV in the morning.

6   My parents ■■□□ _____ go out with their friends.

2 Rewrite the sentences. Add the word in brackets.

1   I'm busy on Saturday. (often)
    I'm often busy on Saturdays.

2   Kit helps me at home. (often)
    _____

3   Uncle Roberto visits me. (sometimes)
    _____

4   I cook dinner. (never)
    _____

5   Kit is happy. (always)
    _____

6   Kit and I have fun. (usually)
    _____

3 Complete the days of week. Then number them in the correct order.

We __ __ esday
__ue__day
1 Monday
Sat__ __day
__u__day
Th__r__day
__r__day

4 Look at the information about Tom and write sentences.

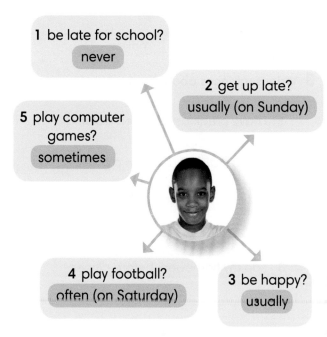

1 be late for school?
   never

2 get up late?
   usually (on Sunday)

5 play computer games?
   sometimes

4 play football?
   often (on Saturday)

3 be happy?
   usually

1   Tom _is never late for school_.
2   He _____.
3   He _____.
4   He _____.
5   He _____.

5 Look at the information about Tom and write sentences for you.

1   I _____ late for school.
2   _____
3   _____
4   _____
5   _____

I can tell the time.

🔊 **14 Telling the time**

A: What time is it?

B: It's 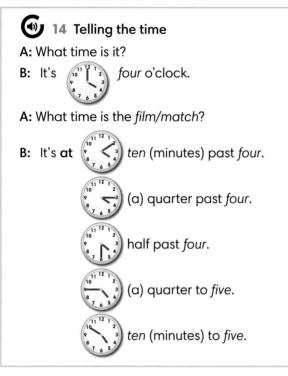 *four* o'clock.

A: What time is the *film/match*?

B: It's **at** ten (minutes) past *four*.

(a) quarter past *four*.

half past *four*.

(a) quarter to *five*.

ten (minutes) to *five*.

1 Match clocks a–h to expressions 1–8.

 a
 b
 c
 d
 e
 f
 g
 h

1 [b] six o'clock
2 [ ] (a) quarter to five
3 [ ] half past two
4 [ ] five to one
5 [e] (a) quarter past one
6 [ ] five past five
7 [ ] twenty to nine
8 [ ] ten past nine

2 Complete the sequences.

1 twelve o'clock – five past twelve – ¹*ten past twelve*
– quarter past twelve – ² _____ –
twenty-five past twelve –
³ _____

2 half past two – ⁴ _____ –
twenty to three – ⁵ _____ –
ten to three – ⁶ _____ –
three o'clock

3 Look at the TV schedule. Then complete the questions and answers.

18:00	18:35	19:05	19:15	19:50
Pet Time	Super Girl	Happy Days	That's Magic	The Great Big Talent Show

1 A: What time is *Pet Time*?
  B: *It's at six o'clock.*
2 A: What time is *That's Magic*?
  B: _____
3 A: _____ ?
  B: It's at five past seven.
4 A: _____ ?
  B: It's at twenty-five to seven.
5 A: What time is *the Great Big Talent Show*?
  B: _____
6 A: OK. _____ now?
  B: It's five to six. Hurry up!

4 Put the dialogue in the correct order.

a [1] What time is it, Mandy?
b [ ] No, I'm not. I'm late for my music lesson.
c [ ] It's at quarter to six. Bye!
d [ ] It's half past five. Oh no!
e [ ] What's wrong? Are you OK?
f [ ] Oh dear. What time is your music lesson?

5 Complete the sentences for you.

1 I get up at _____ .
2 I have breakfast at _____ .
3 I go to school at _____ .
4 I do my homework at _____ .
5 I go to bed at _____ .

6.5 | READING and VOCABULARY | Months

I can understand texts about teenagers' daily routines.

Hi. I'm Mike. I'm twelve and I'm American. I live in New York. My school is very big. I like sport. I'm not very good at Art but I love it. I have lunch in the classroom. I usually have pizza! After school I always hang out with my friends. We sometimes play basketball or we go to the park.

My name is Dasha and I'm eleven. I'm from Moscow, in Russia. I go to a special school. It's a ballet school! After breakfast we have lessons. My favourite lessons are Maths and English. Then we have lunch. I often have pancakes! After lunch we dance. I'm always busy.

1 Read the texts. Match photos A–F to Mike or Dasha.

1 Mike [B] [ ] [ ]
2 Dasha [ ] [ ] [ ]

 A

 B

 C

 D

 E

 F

2 Read the texts again. Circle T (true) or F (false).

1 Mike likes Art. (T)/ F
2 He eats pizza in the classroom. T / F
3 He never goes to the park after school. T / F
4 Dasha likes Maths. T / F
5 She has pancakes every day. T / F
6 She dances before lunch. T / F

3 Read the texts again. Complete the sentences with one or two words in each gap.

1 Mike goes to a _____ school.
2 He plays basketball with _____.
3 Dasha _____ after breakfast.
4 She is always _____.

4 Complete the names of the months.

1 D e c e m b e r
2 Fe _ r _ a _ y
3 J _ n _
4 O _ _ o _ er
5 A _ r _ l
6 A _ g _ _ t

5 Complete with the words in Exercise 4.

January	¹_____	March
²_____	May	³_____
July	⁴_____	September
⁵_____	November	⁶*December*

I can understand and write short texts about a typical day on holiday.

1 🔊 **15 Listen to Andy and complete the notes.**

Andy's holidays

Country: ¹ *Spain*
Aunt's nationality: ² _____
Aunt's job: ³ _____
Favourite place: ⁴ _____
Favourite game: ⁵ _____

2 🔊 **15 Listen again. Circle the correct word.**

1 Andy (always)/ *usually* goes on holiday in August.
2 After breakfast they *usually / often* go to the beach.
3 They *always / often* have a picnic on the beach.
4 They *usually / often* go to bed after lunch.
5 He *always / never* gets up early.

3 Circle *before* and *after* in Jane's blog post.

We never go to school in August. It's a holiday! I get up late. I often play computer games (before) breakfast. I never have breakfast in bed. I have it in the kitchen. After breakfast I often hang out with friends. Before dinner I sometimes help my parents. I usually watch TV after dinner. I often go to bed late.

4 Read the blog again. Put the activities in the boxes in the correct order.

> ~~get up~~ hang out with friends
> have breakfast play computer games

Before lunch

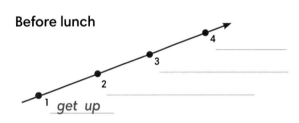

1 *get up*
2 _____
3 _____
4 _____

> go to bed have dinner
> help my parents watch TV

After lunch

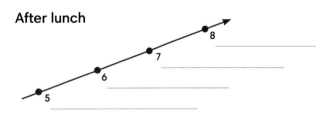

5 _____
6 _____
7 _____
8 _____

5 Write about your typical holiday day. Use *before* and *after*.

_____
_____
_____
_____
_____
_____
_____

I can talk and write about things I can do on the Internet.

1 Match 1–6 to a–f to make expressions.

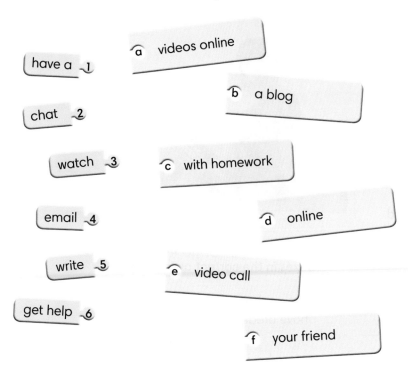

have a — 1
chat — 2
watch — 3
email — 4
write — 5
get help — 6

a videos online
b a blog
c with homework
d online
e video call
f your friend

2 What do the people do on the Internet? Look at the pictures and complete the sentences.

1 My cousin lives in the USA. We often have a v _i_ _d_ _e_ o call at the weekend.

2 Danny loves his granny. He e _ _ _ _ _ her every week.

3 Linda and Lizzie usually watch videos o _ _ _ _ _ _ at the weekend.

4 Brian sometimes c _ _ _ _ _ to people online.

5 Angela sometimes g _ _ _ _ help with her homework.

6 Roger often reads this b _ _ _. It's very interesting!

3 Complete the dialogues. Use sentences A–F in the box.

A Do you chat online?
B Yes, I often get help with my homework online.
C No, they don't! They text them.
D On Saturday. We can have a video call.
E Do all his friends read it?
F No, I never watch it, but I often watch videos online.

1 A When can I see you again?
  B [D]
2 A Do you watch TV a lot?
  B ☐
3 A Tom writes his blog every day. It's very funny!
  B ☐
4 A My best friends don't live in the UK, but we chat every day.
  B ☐
5 A Do young people often email their friends?
  B ☐
6 A Do you need the Internet for your school work?
  B ☐

SELF-ASSESSMENT

For each learning objective, tick (✓) the box that best matches your ability.

☺☺ = I understand and can help a friend.　　☹ = I understand but have some questions.

☺ = I understand and can do it by myself.　　☹☹ = I do not understand.

		☺☺	☺	☹	☹☹	Need help?	Now try ...
6.1	Vocabulary					Students' Book pp. 80–81 Workbook p. 58	Ex. 1–2, p. 66
6.2	Grammar					Students' Book pp. 82–83 Workbook p. 59	Ex. 3, p. 66
6.3	Grammar					Students' Book pp. 84–85 Workbook p. 60	Ex. 4, p. 66
6.4	Communication					Students' Book p. 86 Workbook p. 61	Ex. 5, p. 66
6.5	Reading and Vocabulary					Students' Book p. 87 Workbook p. 62	
6.6	Listening and Writing					Students' Book p. 88 Workbook p. 63	
6.7	CLIL					Students' Book p. 89 Workbook p. 64	

6.1　I can talk about daily activities.
6.2　I can use the Present Simple in affirmative sentences.
6.3　I can use adverbs of frequency.
6.4　I can tell the time.
6.5　I can understand texts about teenagers' daily routines.
6.6　I can understand and write short texts about a typical day on holiday.
6.7　I can talk and write about things I can do on the Internet.

What can you remember from this unit?

New words I learned (the words you most want to remember from this unit)	**Expressions and phrases I liked** (any expressions or phrases you think sound nice, useful or funny)	**English I heard or read outside class** (e.g. from websites, books, adverts, films, music)

SELF-CHECK

Vocabulary

1 Complete the sentences with one word in each gap.

0 In the morning, I **get** up at seven o'clock.

1 We _____ lessons all day.

2 After school, I _____ out with friends.

3 We _____ computer games on Saturdays.

4 Before bed, I _____ TV.

5 At night, I _____ to bed at 9.

/5

2 Complete the sequences.

0	January	*February*	March
1	July		September
2	Friday		Sunday
3	October		December
4	March		May
5	Tuesday		Thursday

/5

Grammar

3 Complete the sentences. Put the verbs in the correct form.

0 Tom *gets up* (get up) early.

1 We _____ (go) to a big school.

2 Sally _____ (like) chocolate ice cream.

3 Tim _____ (tidy) his room every day.

4 They _____ (live) in London.

5 I _____ (have) lunch in the park.

/5

4 Rewrite the sentences. Add the word in brackets.

0 They walk to school. (always)
They always walk to school.

1 I am busy in the afternoon. (usually)

_____

2 We play tennis. (never)

_____

3 Mum watches TV. (sometimes)

_____

4 He is late for school. (always)

_____

5 My cat sleeps on my bed. (often)

_____

/5

Communication

5 Complete the dialogue with one word in each gap.

1 A: What ⁰*time* is lunch?
  B: It's at half ¹_____ twelve.

2 A: What time ²_____ it?
  B: It's ten ³_____ to five.

3 A: What time is the film?
  B: It's ⁴_____ six o'⁵_____.

/5

Vocabulary /10

Grammar /10

Communication /5

Your total score /25

Reading and Writing

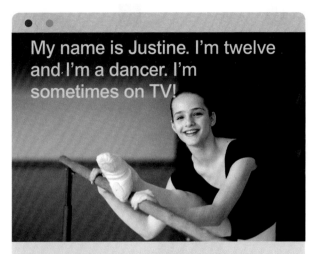

My name is Justine. I'm twelve and I'm a dancer. I'm sometimes on TV!

My week

I always get up at half past six. I have breakfast and then I go to school. My school is a special dancing school. We have dancing lessons after school on Mondays, Wednesdays and Fridays. We run, jump and dance! We often make videos. That's very cool. Then I go home and do my homework. I have dinner and speak to my family. I usually go to bed at half past nine.

At the weekend I usually hang out with my best friend, Madalena. We are classmates. We talk about our lessons and watch videos about our favourite dancers.

1 Read the text. What is it about? Circle the correct answer.

A   A girl
B   A school   ☐ /1

2 Read the text again. Circle T (true) or F (false).

0   Justine can dance.   Ⓣ/ F
1   Justine gets up early.   T / F
2   Justine has breakfast at home.   T / F
3   Her dancing lessons are on Thursdays. T / F
4   The students never make videos
    in their dancing lessons.   T / F
5   Madalena isn't Justine's sister.   T / F
6   Justine and Madalena make videos
    at the weekend.   T / F

                                               ☐ /6

3 Write five sentences about what Alice usually does on Mondays.

0   get up ⸤07:15⸥
1   have breakfast ⸤08:00⸥
2   go to school ⸤08:30⸥
3   have lessons all day!
4   do homework ⸤17:00⸥
5   have dinner at granny's house ⸤18:45⸥

0   *Alice gets up at quarter past seven.*
1   _____
2   _____
3   _____
4   _____
5   _____

                                               ☐ /5

Listening

4 🔊 16 Julie is with her mum's friend, Mrs Williams. Mrs Williams has got some family photos. Listen and match names 0–4 to a–e to make sentences.

0   Rob   ⸤ b ⸥   a   can cook cupcakes.
1   Ann   ☐   b   can play basketball.
2   Barney ☐   c   goes swimming on Saturday.
3   Karen   ☐   d   is Barney's friend.
4   May   ☐   e   is twelve.

                                               ☐ /4

Communication

5 Complete the dialogues with one word in each gap.

0   **Alex:** Can you sing?
    Kim: *Yes*, I can!
1   **Alex:** Let's go to Music Club.
    Kim: It's not a good _____.
2   **Alex:** I know! We can go to the cinema!
    Kim: _____ do that!
3   **Alex:** What time is the film?
    Kim: It's _____ half past five.
4   **Alex:** Let's ask Michelle to come.
    Kim: OK, we _____ phone her.

                                               ☐ /4

Reading and Writing   ☐ /12
Listening   ☐ /4
Communication   ☐ /4
Your total score   ☐ /20

7

Animals

I can talk about animals.

1 Match animals a–h with words 1–8.

a  b  c

d  e  f

g  h

1 [d] crocodile	5 [ ] lion
2 [ ] frog	6 [ ] monkey
3 [ ] butterfly	7 [ ] snake
4 [ ] kangaroo	8 [ ] whale

2 Which animal is different? Circle the odd one out. Match it to the correct reason.

1 [c] fish crocodile frog (spider)   a It lives in water.
2 [ ] snake butterfly bird fly   b It can fly.
3 [ ] elephant fish monkey tiger   c It can't swim.
4 [ ] lion tiger giraffe bird   d It can't fly.
5 [ ] tiger whale snake fish   e It's got legs.

3 Circle the correct word.

1 *Frogs /* (*Crocodiles*) have got big mouths.
2 *Whales / Frogs* live in the sea.
3 *Spiders / Snakes* are very long.
4 *Tigers / Birds* can fly.
5 *Frogs / Snakes* can jump.
6 *Spiders / Lions* have got eight legs.
7 *Kangaroos / Monkeys* can climb trees.

4 What can animals do? Write two animals under each verb. Use words in Exercise 2.

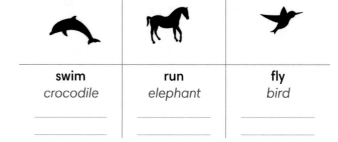

swim	run	fly
crocodile	*elephant*	*bird*
___	___	___

I can use the negative form of the Present Simple and talk about pets.

1 Circle the correct answer.

1 My parents (don't)/ doesn't play computer games.
2 I don't / doesn't get up early on Saturday.
3 Lucy don't / doesn't like cats.
4 We don't / doesn't hang out on Monday.
5 Josh don't / doesn't go to school by bike.
6 We don't / doesn't have lessons on Sunday.
7 You don't / doesn't tidy your bedroom every morning.
8 Elephants don't / doesn't eat fish.

2 Complete the sentences. Put the verbs in the correct form.

1 My pet doesn't like (not like) chocolate.
2 I _____ (not tidy) my room every day.
3 We _____ (not watch) TV before dinner.
4 My little sister _____ (not go) to school.
5 You _____ (not like) pop music.
6 My cousin _____ (not speak) French.

3 Write affirmative (✓) or negative (✗) sentences.

1 my puppy / ✓ like / TV
   My puppy likes TV.
2 cats / ✗ eat / cupcakes
   Cats don't eat cupcakes.
3 my friend / ✓ play / in the garden
   _____
4 my sister / ✗ tidy / her bedroom
   _____
5 Joe and Amy / ✓ hang out / after school
   _____
6 we / ✗ go to school / on Sunday
   _____

4 Look at the table. Correct the sentences.

	get up early	play computer games	listen to classical music
Jen	✗	✔	✗
Alex	✗	✔	✔
Mum	✔	✗	✔
Dad	✗	✗	✔

1 Jen, Alex and dad get up early.
   Jen, Alex and dad don't get up early.
2 Dad gets up early.
   _____
3 Jen and Alex don't play computer games.
   _____
4 Mum and dad play computer games.
   _____
5 Mum doesn't listen to classical music.
   _____
6 Jen listens to classical music.
   _____

5 Match animals a–h to sentences 1–8.

1 [a] It's got small ears.   a a hamster
2 [ ] It can fly.   b a tortoise
3 [ ] It lives in water.   c a parrot
4 [ ] It's got long ears.   d a rabbit
5 [ ] It's got a long body.   e a goldfish
6 [ ] It doesn't walk fast!   f an iguana
7 [ ] Its babies are puppies.   g a dog

6 Complete the sentences for you.

1 On Wednesday, I _____ .

2 On Sunday, I don't _____ .

3 On Monday, my friend _____ .

4 On Saturday, my friend doesn't _____ .

7.3 GRAMMAR Present Simple questions and short answers

I can ask and answer questions in the Present Simple.

1 Circle the correct word.

1 (Do)/ Does you know Mari?
2 Do / Does Tom live in a house with a garden?
3 Do / Does your friends speak English?
4 Do / Does your mum make nice cakes?
5 Do / Does I sing well?
6 Do / Does you and your sister like cats?

2 Match answers a–f to the questions in Exercise 1.

a ☐ Yes, she does.
b ☐ No, you don't.
c ☐1 Yes, I do.
d ☐ Yes, we do.
e ☐ No, they don't.
f ☐ Yes, he does.

3 Complete the dialogue with do, does, don't or doesn't.

Reporter: ¹<u>Do</u> you speak any foreign languages, Superdug?
Superdug: No, I ²_____ .
Reporter: ³_____ Kit speak any foreign languages?
Superdug: Yes, she ⁴_____ .
Reporter: ⁵_____ you and Kit work together?
Superdug: Yes, we ⁶_____ .

4 Write questions.

1 Suzie goes to school at eight o'clock.
Does Suzie go to school at eight o'clock?
2 Mike plays football at school.
_____
3 Lucy has piano lessons on Monday.
_____
4 Dave watches DVDs to relax.
_____
5 Rosie tidies her bedroom on Saturday.
_____

5 Write questions.

1 you / speak Chinese?
Do you speak Chinese?
2 you / like chocolate?
_____
3 your teacher / ride a bike to school?
_____
4 your friends / play football on Saturday?
_____
5 you / hang out with your friends at the weekend?
_____
6 your dad / go to the gym?
_____

6 Answer the questions in Exercise 5 for you.

1 *No, I don't.*
2 _____
3 _____
4 _____
5 _____
6 _____

7 Complete the questions. Use do/does and the verbs below.

| do   drink   go   have   play   speak |

1 A: What <u>do</u> you _____ after school?
  B: I usually hang out with my friends.
2 A: What _____ Sandra _____ for dinner on Fridays?
  B: Pizza!
3 A: When _____ they _____ tennis?
  B: At the weekend.
4 A: What _____ your pet _____ ?
  B: Water, of course.
5 A: What time _____ you _____ to bed?
  B: At ten o'clock.
6 A: _____ your best friend _____ any foreign languages?
  B: Yes! My best friend is French!

I can buy a ticket.

🔊 **17** Buying a ticket

A: Can I help you?
B: Can I have *one ticket / two tickets* to the zoo, please?
A: That's eighteen pounds fifty.
B: Here you are.
A: *Here's your ticket. / Here are your tickets.*
B: Thanks.

1 Read the dialogue and circle the correct answer.

A: Can I help you?
B: ¹*Can I have / Would you like* a ticket to the museum, please?
A: ²*Would / Do* you like a guide?
B: No, ³*thanks / please.*
A: That's £8.50, please.
B: Here ⁴*are you / you are.*
A: ⁵*They're / Here are* your tickets.
B: Thank you.

2 Complete the dialogue with the phrases below.

> and here's   can I have   can I help   here
> you are   that's   would you like

Assistant: ¹*Can I help* you?
Customer: Yes please. ²_____ a sandwich, please?
Assistant: Yes, OK. ³_____ a drink too?
Customer: Yes please. I'd like some water
Assistant: ⁴_____ £4.25, please.
Customer: ⁵_____.
Assistant: Thank you. ⁶_____ your sandwich.

3 Complete the table.

1		£5.50	*five pounds fifty*
2		£ _____	two pounds fifty
3		£8.90	_____
4		£ _____	four pounds thirty
5		£1.20	_____

4 Complete the dialogue with one word in each gap.

A: Hello. ¹*Can* I help you?
B: Hi. Can I ²_____ two tickets for the cinema, ³_____?
A: Sure. Would you ⁴_____ a bag of popcorn?
B: ⁵_____, please. Good idea!
A: ⁶_____ £15, please.
B: ⁷_____ you are.
A: Here ⁸_____ your tickets and ⁹_____'s the popcorn. Enjoy the film!
B: Thanks.

I can understand a text about sharks.

ALL ABOUT ... SHARKS

Are all sharks dangerous to people?
No, not all sharks are dangerous to us, but we are very dangerous to sharks! Why? Sharks don't often eat people, but in some countries people eat sharks.

What do sharks usually eat?
They eat fish and other sea animals.
They sometimes eat other sharks.

Are they clever? What can they do?
Sharks are strong and they can swim fast.
They can see and smell under water very well.

Can they hear?
Good question. It's amazing. They haven't got ears like our ears, but they can hear fish from hundreds of kilometres away!

1 Look at the photos. Circle T (true) or F (false).

1 fast   (T)/ F

2 strong   T / F

3 dangerous   T / F

4 cute   T / F

5 ugly   T / F

6 slow   T / F

2 Which words describe sharks? Tick (✓) for *yes* and put a cross (✗) for *no*.

dangerous ✓   fast ☐   strong ☐
lots of teeth ☐   long body ☐
cute face ☐   big ears ☐

3 Read the text. Circle the correct answer.
1 Sharks are (sometimes) / always dangerous to people.
2 People *are / aren't* a problem for sharks.
3 Sharks don't often eat *sea animals / other sharks*.
4 They *have got / haven't got* very good eyes.
5 They *can / can't* hear very well.

4 Read the text again. Answer the questions.
1 What do sharks usually eat?
_____
2 Do they often eat people?
_____
3 Can they smell well?
_____
4 What can they hear?
_____

I can understand and write short texts about pets.

1 🔊 18 Listen to Emma and Ted. Tick (✓) the pets Emma has got.

A ☐

B ☐

C ☐

2 🔊 18 Listen again. Answer the questions.

1 Where are the pets?
They're in Emma's bedroom.

2 Are they brothers or sisters?
_____

3 What colour is Ted's favourite pet?
_____

4 What do they need every day?
_____

5 Where does their special food come from?
_____

3 🔊 18 Listen again. Circle the correct answer.

1 There are *two* / *three* pets.
2 Emma says they *are* / *aren't* easy to look after.
3 They *like* / *don't like* fruit.
4 Ted has got some *hamsters* / *rabbits*.

4 Read the email. Circle the correct answer.

✉ ✕

Hi Sam,

I know you like cats. Well, our cat has got some kittens. Would you like one? They are cute. Three are black, two are black and white and one is grey. They haven't got names. They are very young. They're very friendly too!

Kittens eat special kitten food but they don't eat a lot. They drink water but milk isn't good for them.

Kittens are easy to look after. They don't go for walks and they sleep a lot.

Can you ask your mum and dad? Let me know.

Ben

1 Does Sam like cats?
(*Yes, he does.*) / *No, he doesn't.*
2 How many kittens are there?
There are three. / *There are six.*
3 Have they got names?
Yes, they have. / *No, they haven't.*
4 Do they eat a lot?
Yes, they do. / *No, they don't.*
5 Can Sam have a kitten?
Yes, he can. / *We don't know.*

5 You have got some puppies. Write an email to a friend and offer him/her one of them. Use the words in the box or your own ideas.

black and brown
cute, funny, friendly
✓ special puppy food
✓ water ✗ milk
sleep and play

≡ ↻

start the email _____

describe the puppies _____
_____

food and drink? _____

do? _____

ask mum and dad? _____
_____

end the email _____

I can talk and write about where animals live.

1 Find seven environment words. Then look at the photos and complete the sentences.

A	O	S	E	A	D	L
T	R	E	E	S	A	A
R	H	G	Y	F	M	N
F	O	R	P	O	N	D
K	L	O	B	R	E	P
V	E	U	O	E	A	W
C	E	N	T	S	U	A
N	Q	D	I	T	G	B

1 Some animals live in the _sea_.

2 Some animals live on _____.

3 Some animals live in a _____.

4 Some animals live in the _____.

5 Some animals live in a _____ in the _____.

6 Some animals live in _____.

2 Where do these animals live? Write S (sea) or L (land).

1 — L
2 — ☐
3 — ☐
4 — ☐
5 — ☐
6 — ☐
7 — ☐
8 — ☐

3 Complete the sentences.

1 Whales and fish live in the s e a.

2 Frogs and small fish live in a _ _ _ _.

3 Rabbits and groundhogs live in a hole in the _ _ _ _ _ _.

4 Elephants and tigers live in the _ _ _ _ _ _.

5 Monkeys and birds live in _ _ _ _ _.

SELF-ASSESSMENT

For each learning objective, tick (✓) the box that best matches your ability.

☺☺ = I understand and can help a friend.   ☹ = I understand but have some questions.

☺ = I understand and can do it by myself.   ☹☹ = I do not understand.

		☺☺	☺	☹	☹☹	Need help?	Now try …
1.1	Vocabulary					Students' Book pp. 94–95 Workbook p. 68	Ex. 1–2, p. 76
1.2	Grammar					Students' Book pp. 96–97 Workbook p. 69	Ex. 3, p. 76
1.3	Grammar					Students' Book pp. 98–99 Workbook p. 70	Ex. 4, p. 76
1.4	Communication					Students' Book p. 100 Workbook p. 71	Ex. 5, p. 76
1.5	Reading and Vocabulary					Students' Book p. 101 Workbook p. 72	
1.6	Listening and Writing					Students' Book p. 102 Workbook p. 73	
1.7	CLIL					Students' Book p. 103 Workbook p. 74	

7.1   I can talk about animals.
7.2   I can use the negative form of the Present Simple and talk about pets.
7.3   I can ask and answer questions in the Present Simple.
7.4   I can buy a ticket.
7.5   I can understand a text about sharks.
7.6   I can understand and write short texts about pets.
7.7   I can talk and write about where animals live.

What can you remember from this unit?

New words I learned (the words you most want to remember from this unit)	**Expressions and phrases I liked** (any expressions or phrases you think sound nice, useful or funny)	**English I heard or read outside class** (e.g. from websites, books, adverts, films, music)

SELF-CHECK

Vocabulary

1 Match the word fragments to make pet words.

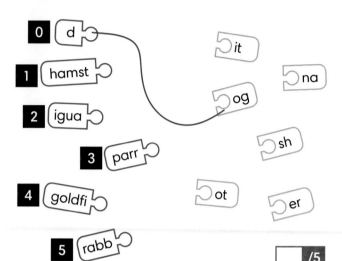

0	d
1	hamst
2	igua
3	parr
4	goldfi
5	rabb

it
na
og
sh
ot
er

/5

2 Complete the sentences.

0 a c<u>ute</u> c<u>a</u>t   1 a f _ _ t b _ _ d

2 a d _ _ ge _ _ us   3 a s _ _ w
   l _ _ n   t _ _ to _ _ e

4 an u _ _ y f _ _ g   5 a st _ _ _ g
                               e _ _ ph _ _ t

/5

Grammar

3 Complete the sentences. Put the verbs in the correct form.

0 I *don't get up* (not get up) early at weekends.
1 My friend _____ (not sing) in a band.
2 We _____ (not live) in a big house.
3 Ella _____ (not like) vegetables.
4 I _____ (not speak) French very well.
5 Mum and dad _____ (not want) a pet snake.

/5

4 Write questions. Answer yes (✓) or no (✗). Use short answers.

1 I / speak good English?
   A: ⁰*Do I speak good English?*
   B: ✔ ⁰⁰*Yes, you do.*
2 Tom / wear jeans to school?
   A: ¹ _____
   B: ✗ ² _____
3 your friends / like football?
   A: ³ _____
   B: ✔ ⁴ _____
4 your granny / visit you every week?
   A: ⁵ _____
   B: ✗ ⁶ _____

/5

Communication

5 Complete the dialogue with one word in each gap

A: Hello, ⁰*can* I help ¹ _____ ?
B: Can I ² _____ two tickets, ³ _____ ?
A: Yes, ⁴ _____ fifteen pounds fifty.
B: Here you are.
A: Here ⁵ _____ your tickets.

/5

Vocabulary	/10
Grammar	/10
Communication	/5
Your total score	/25

1 Look at the photos and do the puzzle.

(Crossword grid with numbered cells 1, 2, 3, 4, 5, 6, 7)

Down

1 d_____

2  ax_____

4  c_____

5 r_____

Across

3  pygmy h_____

6 t_____

7 f_____

2 Complete the descriptions with the words below.

> cute ears funny legs live ~~popular~~ quiet run scary small

1 Dogs are very **popular** pets. Some are big and some are _____ . They're very good friends!

2 Tarantulas are _____ and they've got eight legs. They're very _____ animals.

3 Rabbits are cute. They've got long _____ and they can jump and _____ fast.

4 Axolotls have a _____ name! They aren't fish but they _____ in the water.

5 Pygmy hedgehogs are small and very _____ ! They've got short _____ , black eyes and a brown nose.

I like that!

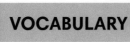

8.1 VOCABULARY Sports

I can talk about sports.

1 Look at the photos. Circle the correct word.

1 (cycling)/ taekwondo   2 hockey / badminton

3 canoeing / windsurfing   4 basketball / volleyball

5 tennis / table tennis   6 ice-skating / roller skating

2 Look at the pictures and label the sports. Use words from Exercise 1.

1 *badminton*   4 _____
2 _____   5 _____
3 _____   6 _____

3 Circle the correct word.

1 (go)/ play ice-skating   6 go / play swimming
2 do / go cycling   7 do / go canoeing
3 go / do taekwondo   8 play / go volleyball
4 play / go tennis   9 go / do snowboarding
5 do / play football   10 play / do badminton

4 Match 1–6 to a–f.

1 [d] I sometimes play   a hockey with his friends.
2 [ ] George does   b ice-skating.
3 [ ] Do you go   c snowboarding with your friends?
4 [ ] My brother plays   d badminton with my dad.
5 [ ] Sandra never goes   e basketball at school?
6 [ ] Do you often play   f taekwondo every Monday.

8.2 **GRAMMAR** *love / like / don't like / hate + -ing*; object pronouns

I can use verbs *love / like / don't like / hate + -ing* and use object pronouns.

1 Complete the sentences. Put the verbs in the correct form. Who is it? Write Jen, Alex, Lucas or Lian.

1 This person loves **playing** (play) the guitar.
  Who? *Lucas*
2 This person likes _____ (make) cupcakes.
  Who? _____
3 This person hates _____ (get up) early and _____ (cook).
  Who? _____
4 This person likes _____ (skateboard) and _____ (climb).
  Who? _____

2 Complete the sentences with the words below. There is one extra word.

| doesn't like | don't like | ~~hate~~ |
| hates | like | likes | love | loves |

1 We ☹️☹️ ____hate____ rock climbing.
2 My parents 🙂 _____ windsurfing.
3 Ann ☹️ _____ playing football.
4 My grandad 🙂🙂 _____ cooking.
5 My friends ☹️ _____ getting up early.
6 I 🙂🙂 _____ cycling.
7 Mark 🙂 _____ playing basketball.

3 Look at the pictures and write sentences. Use the words in the box below.

climb   eat   ~~get~~   sleep

1 ☹️☹️
  My cat *hates getting* wet.

2 🙂
  She _____ fish for lunch.

3 🙂🙂
  She _____ trees in the garden.

4 ☹️
  She _____ in her bed. She likes *my* bed!

4 Complete the sentences with object pronouns.

1 Emma is nice. I like ____her____ .
2 Ice-skating is fun. I love _____ .
3 You are great at football. I like watching _____ .
4 Amy and Tom are my best friends. I like _____ .
5 Tom is my baby brother. I love _____ .
6 We're good at dancing. Watch _____ !

5 Complete the dialogue with the words below.

~~doing~~   hate   her   me   playing   plays   she

A: What does your sister like ¹*doing* at the weekend?
B: Monica loves sports. ² _____ often goes swimming or she ³ _____ tennis.
A: Do you play tennis with ⁴ _____ ?
B: No. I ⁵ _____ it. I love ⁶ _____ football! Do you want to play with ⁷ _____ and my friends?

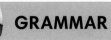

I can ask detailed questions.

1 Read the questions and circle the correct answer.

1 A: When is the football game?
 B: *It's great.* / *(It's on Saturday)*.

2 A: Where is my mobile phone?
 B: *It's on the table.* / *It's from China.*

3 A: Whose bike is in front of the house?
 B: *The bike is green.* / *It's my mum's bike.*

4 A: How many friends have you got?
 B: *Five.* / *Five years old.*

5 A: What is in your bag?
 B: *It's next to the desk.* / *There's a notebook.*

6 A: Who is your English teacher?
 B: *Mr Evans is here.* / *It's Mr Evans.*

2 Look at the picture and circle the correct word.

1 A: *(Where)* / *When* is Dug?
 B: He's in a shopping centre.

2 A: *Who* / *Whose* is the woman?
 B: She's Irina Peters.

3 A: *Who* / *What* is her sport?
 B: It's tennis.

4 A: *What* / *Who* does Dug want?
 B: He wants her autograph.

5 A: *How many* / *When* mobile phones can you see?
 B: Two.

3 Match 1–6 to a–f to make questions.

1 Who | d |
2 What | |
3 Where | |
4 How many | |
5 When | |
6 Whose | |

a do you live?
b is in your bag?
c sisters have you got?
d is your best friend?
e skateboard is that?
f is your birthday?

4 Complete the dialogue with the words below.

| How many ~~What~~ When Where Who Whose

A: ¹*What*'s your name?
B: Baris.
A: ² _____ are you from?
B: I'm from Turkey, but I live in London now.
A: ³ _____ friends have you got in London?
B: A lot! Six or seven.
A: ⁴ _____ is your best friend?
B: Jacob. He's my classmate. We want to go to a party today.
A: ⁵ _____ party is it?
B: It's my sister's party! It's her birthday!
A: ⁶ _____ is the party?
B: It's at five o'clock.

5 Write questions.

1 how many classmates / you / have got?
 How many classmates have you got?
2 when / you / go to bed on Mondays?
 _____
3 where / your friends / hang out?
 _____
4 what / be / your favourite sport?
 _____
5 who / be / your favourite singer?
 _____

6 Write your answers to the questions in Exercise 4.

1 *I've got _____ classmates.*
2 _____
3 _____
4 _____
5 _____

COMMUNICATION The weather

I can talk about the weather.

◄))) 19 Talking about the weather

A: What's the weather like?

B: It's *cloudy/cold/hot/rainy/snowy/sunny/ warm/windy.*

It's *cold/hot/rainy/sunny* in *winter/summer/ autumn/spring.*

1 Put the sentences in the dialogue in the correct order.

a ☐ Oh dear. That's horrible.

b ☐ It's cold and snowy here.

c ☐ Well, I hope it's snowy in Scotland too!

d ☐ *1* Hi, Mandy. Is the weather nice in Scotland?

e ☐ No, it isn't. It's rainy and cold!

f ☐ Yes, it's really horrible. What's the weather like in France?

2 Label the pictures.

1 *sunny* 2 _____ 3 _____

4 _____ 5 _____ 6 _____

7 _____ 8 _____

3 Complete the sentences with weather words.

1 It's *h o t*. Let's go swimming.

2 It's very c _ _ _ . Wear a coat.

3 It's w _ _ _ _ . Let's go windsurfing.

4 It's r _ _ _ _ . Let's stay at home.

5 It's s _ _ _ _ . Let's go snowboarding.

6 It's w _ _ _ . Wear a T-shirt.

4 Label the photos. Use the words in the box.

autumn   spring   summer   winter

1 _____   2 _____

3 _____   4 _____

5 Read and circle the correct word.

1 It's sometimes hot in (summer)/ winter.

2 It's *often / never* warm in spring.

3 It's always cold in *winter / spring.*

4 It's often rainy and *cloudy / sunny* in autumn.

5 It's never snowy in *winter / summer.*

6 Complete the dialogue with the words below.

hope   hot   like   rainy   wet   ~~what~~

A: Hi, ¹*what*'s the weather ² _____ in New York today?

B: It's windy and ³ _____ . I've got an umbrella!

A: I hate getting ⁴ _____ !

B: Me too! I ⁵ _____ it's sunny and ⁶ _____ tomorrow.

I can understand short texts about healthy habits.

Sam is thirteen. He likes getting up early but he goes to bed very late. He loves sports. He goes swimming before school. After school he plays football. At the weekend he goes cycling with his friends. Sam's sister Tammy is eleven. She doesn't like sport and she never does exercise. She likes reading and cooking. She goes to bed at ten and she gets up at half past six.

Sam loves cakes and chocolate and he often eats pizza and chips, but Tammy doesn't usually eat them. Sam doesn't like fruit and he hates vegetables, but Tammy loves them. Tammy likes chocolate but she doesn't eat it a lot. Sam usually drinks cola, but Tammy doesn't like it. She drinks fruit juice or water. Who is healthy, Tammy or Sam?

1 Read the text. Circle the correct word.

	Sam	Tammy
do exercise	1 *often / sometimes*	2 *usually / never*
eat healthy food	3 *yes / no*	4 *yes / no*

2 Read the text again. Answer the questions.

1 What exercise does Sam do in the morning?
   He goes swimming.

2 When does Tammy do exercise?
   _____

3 What does Tammy like doing?
   _____

4 What does Sam like eating?
   _____

5 Does Tammy like fruit and vegetables?
   _____

6 What does Sam usually drink?
   _____

3 Match 1–6 to a–f.

1 [d] eat   a your teeth
2 [ ] drink   b exercise
3 [ ] do   c friends
4 [ ] brush   d fruit and
5 [ ] have   vegetables
6 [ ] go   e to bed early
                     f a lot of water

4 Look at the photos. Complete the text with expressions in Exercise 3.

I always ¹*brush* my ²_____ in the morning and after dinner. I eat a lot of ³_____ and ⁴_____ . I love apples and oranges. I ⁵_____ some ⁶_____ every week. I often go cycling or swimming. I usually ⁷_____ to ⁸_____ early, at eight.

I can understand and write short texts about healthy habits.

1 Match the photos to the topics.

☐ food   ☐ sleep   ☐ exercise

A

B

C

2 🔊 **20** Listen to the dialogue. Match the questions to the topics in Exercise 1.

Question 1: _____

Question 2: _____

Question 3: _____

3 🔊 **20** Listen again. Complete the notes about Tom.

Question 1

Tom's favourite food is ¹ _chips_ .

He eats a lot of ² _____ and vegetables.

He drinks a lot of ³ _____ .

Question 2

He likes ⁴ _____ .

He always ⁵ _____ to school.

He sometimes goes ⁶ _____ .

Question 3

He goes to bed at ⁷ _____ .

He goes to sleep at ⁸ _____ .

4 Read the text. Correct the underlined mistakes.

Andy ¹~~like~~ _likes_ pizza but he ²<u>don't</u> eat it very often. He ³<u>has always</u> lunch at school. He often eats a sandwich. He likes ⁴<u>read</u> and but he doesn't ⁵<u>likes</u> sport very much. His favourite sport ⁶<u>are</u> swimming. He has swimming lessons on Fridays. Andy goes to bed ⁷<u>in</u> nine because he likes ⁸<u>sleep</u>. He doesn't get up early.

5 Write about May's lifestyle. Use the information in the table.

food and drink?	fruit ☹ vegetables ☺ ☺ a lot of water
exercise?	do taekwondo ☺ play badminton / at the weekend walk to school / always
go to bed? get up?	10:00 / usually 7.30

May doesn't like _____

_____

_____

_____

_____

_____

_____

_____

I can read and talk about sports and sports equipment.

1 Look at the pictures and complete the conversation.

1

2

3

4

5

6

7
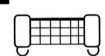

8

Look at my new ¹*bike* and ² _____ !

Cool! Is that a new ³ _____ too?

No, it isn't. It's my brother's. And this is his hockey ⁴ _____ . He loves playing hockey.

I like table tennis. I've got three ⁵ _____ and a lot of ⁶ _____ . But I need a new ⁷ _____ ! Do you play table tennis?

No, I don't. I like playing tennis but I need a new ⁸ _____ !

2 Write the sports. Use the words below.

> tennis   cycling   hockey
> ~~snowboarding~~   swimming   volleyball

1   goggles   snowboard

      snowboarding

2   bike   helmet

      _____

3   stick

  ball   net

      _____

4   goggles   swimming cap

      _____

5   ball

  net   racket

      _____

6   ball   net

      _____

SELF-ASSESSMENT

For each learning objective, tick (✓) the box that best matches your ability.

☺☺ = I understand and can help a friend.   ☹ = I understand but have some questions.

☺ = I understand and can do it by myself.   ☹☹ = I do not understand.

		☺☺	☺	☹	☹☹	Need help?	Now try ...
8.1	Vocabulary					Students' Book pp. 108–109 Workbook p. 78	Ex. 1–2, p. 86
8.2	Grammar					Students' Book pp. 110–111 Workbook p. 79	Ex. 3, p. 86
8.3	Grammar					Students' Book pp. 112–113 Workbook p. 80	Ex. 4, p. 86
8.4	Communication					Students' Book p. 114 Workbook p. 81	Ex. 5, p. 86
8.5	Reading and Vocabulary					Students' Book p. 115 Workbook p. 82	
8.6	Listening and Writing					Students' Book p. 116 Workbook p. 83	
8.7	CLIL					Students' Book p. 117 Workbook p. 84	

8.1   I can talk about sports.

8.2   I can use the verbs *love / like / don't like / hate + -ing* and use object pronouns.

8.3   I can ask detailed questions.

8.4   I can talk about the weather.

8.5   I can understand short texts about healthy habits.

8.6   I can understand and write short texts about healthy habits.

8.7   I can read and talk about sports and sports equipment.

What can you remember from this unit?

New words I learned (the words you most want to remember from this unit)	Expressions and phrases I liked (any expressions or phrases you think sound nice, useful or funny)	English I heard or read outside class (e.g. from websites, books, adverts, films, music)

SELF-CHECK

Vocabulary

1 Find and circle the odd one out.

0 (roller skating) tennis football hockey
1 table tennis taekwondo badminton tennis
2 canoeing windsurfing swimming ice-skating
3 spring January winter summer
4 hot warm autumn sunny
5 snowy cold windy early

2 Look at the photos and complete the words.

0 do e**xercise**

1 b_____ my teeth

2 p_____ badminton

3 g_____ roller skating

4 d_____ a lot of water

5 eat f_____ and vegetables

[ ] /5

Grammar

3 Write sentences.

0 Jack / hate / play / tennis
   Jack hates playing tennis.
1 my sister / not like / roller skate
   _____
2 you / like / swim?
   _____
3 I / love / sing
   _____
4 we / not like / get up / early
   _____
5 your friends / like / eat / pizza?
   _____

[ ] /5

4 Complete the sentences with one word in each gap.

0 A: *Who* is she?
   B: She's my aunt.
1 _____ are you? Are you at school?
2 A: _____ many cakes are there?
   B: Six.
3 Your parents are nice. I like _____.
4 Where's Emma? I can't see _____.
5 Look at that picture! Do you like _____?

[ ] /5

Communication

5 Complete the dialogue with one word in each gap

A: ⁰*What*'s the weather ¹_____?
B: ²_____ cold and rainy.
A: Is ³_____ windy too?
B: Yes, it ⁴_____. I hope it's sunny tomorrow.
A: ⁵_____ too!

[ ] /5

Vocabulary [ ] /10
Grammar [ ] /10
Communication [ ] /5
Your total score [ ] /25

Happy Families

Jimbo, Sasha and Cheeky are our three new babies at City Zoo! Jimbo's ears are big and he's got a very long nose! He loves playing in the water. People at the zoo love him. He's friendly and very cute!

Sasha is a white baby bird. Her mum likes eating insects but Sasha can't eat them. She's too small. She can't fly and she can't run, but her parents can fly and run … on water!

Cheeky is with mum and dad. He's very cute. His face is pink, but his parents' faces are black! He's a baby so he doesn't eat food. He drinks milk. His mum and dad can climb trees but Cheeky can't. He's too small.

Reading and Writing

1 Read the text. Circle T (true) or F (false).

0	Jimbo has got very big eyes.	T / (F)
1	Jimbo likes playing in water.	T / F
2	Jimbo is friendly.	T / F
3	Sasha eats insects.	T / F
4	Sasha can't run on water.	T / F
5	Cheeky's parents have got pink faces.	T / F
6	Cheeky eats a lot of food.	T / F
7	Cheeky's dad can climb trees.	T / F

/7

2 Read the fact file about Jimmy's pet and answer the questions.

Pet	a parrot
Colour	yellow and blue
Food	parrot food, bananas
Abilities	can speak!
Personality	clever, funny
Likes	playing with a ball

0 What is Jimmy's pet?

 It's a parrot.

1 What colour is it?

 _____

2 What does it eat?

 _____

3 What can it do?

 _____

4 What type of personality has it got?

 _____

5 What does it like doing?

 _____

/5

Listening

3 🔊 21 Listen and write.

Sports in my town

0	Name of sports centre:	Hillside
1	Where:	_____ the cinema
2	Number of sports:	_____
3	Team sports:	football, _____ and basketball
4	Type of food in café:	_____ food

/4

Communication

4 Complete dialogue with the words below. There is one extra word.

have   help   here   is   ~~let's~~   that's

A: ⁰*Let's* go to the zoo!

B: Good idea!

C: Can I ¹_____ you?

A: Can I ²_____ two tickets for the zoo, please?

C: ³_____ five pounds forty.

A: ⁴_____ you are.

C: And here are your tickets.

A: Thanks.

/4

Reading and Writing	/12
Listening	/4
Communication	/4
Your total score	/20

SELF-CHECKS ANSWER KEY

Unit 0

Exercise 1
1 12 2 17 3 blue 4 yellow 5 black

Exercise 2
1 ruler 2 notebook 3 chair 4 clock 5 sandwich

Exercise 3
1 They're 2 It's a 3 They're 4 They're 5 It's a

Exercise 4
1 books 2 boxes 3 bins 4 sandwiches 5 trees

Exercise 5
1 please 2 down 3 books 4 pairs 5 up

Unit 1

Exercise 1
1 aunt 2 father 3 brother 4 daughter 5 grandma

Exercise 2
1 park 2 American 3 school 4 France 5 home

Exercise 3
1 are 2 is 3 aren't 4 are 5 am

Exercise 4
1 my 2 We 3 Ben's 4 your 5 Nadia's

Exercise 5
1 is 2 Hello 3 Nice 4 meet 5 too

Unit 2

Exercise 1
1 boring 2 backpack 3 cap 4 top 5 skirt

Exercise 2
1 cap 2 laptop 3 jeans 4 trainers 5 mountain bike

Exercise 3
1 a 2 b 3 b 4 a 5 b

Exercise 4
1 Yes, it is. 2 No, they're not. 3 Yes, we are. 4 No, he isn't. 5 Yes, she is.

Exercise 5
1 d 2 e 3 a 4 f 5 b

Unit 3

Exercise 1
1 armchair 2 window 3 cushion 4 sofa 5 garage

Exercise 2
1 bedroom 2 under 3 kitchen 4 next to 5 fridge

Exercise 3
1 are 2 pen 3 aren't 4 is 5 aren't

Exercise 4
1 isn't 2 Are 3 any 4 aren't 5 a

Exercise 5
1 d 2 e 3 f 4 b 5 a

Unit 4

Exercise 1
1 wavy 2 big 3 nose 4 legs 5 helpful

Exercise 2
1 long 2 straight 3 curly 4 friendly 5 clever

Exercise 3
1 Has 2 got 3 Have 4 haven't 5 hasn't

Exercise 4
1 Their 2 his 3 Her 4 Our 5 its

Exercise 5
1 problem 2 mistake 3 all right 4 It's 5 sure

Unit 5

Exercise 1
1 jump 2 write 3 swim 4 cook 5 run

Exercise 2
1 play 2 make 3 read 4 ride 5 play

Exercise 3
1 can 2 and 3 but 4 can't 5 can

Exercise 4
1 Yes, she can. 2 Can the dogs sing? 3 No, they can't.
4 Can the boy ride his bike? 5 Yes, he can.

Exercise 5
1 can 2 sure 3 can't 4 problem 5 Great

Unit 6

Exercise 1
1 have 2 hang 3 play 4 watch 5 go

Exercise 2
1 August 2 Saturday 3 November 4 April 5 Wednesday

Exercise 3
1 go 2 likes 3 tidies 4 live 5 have

Exercise 4
1 I am usually busy in the afternoon. 2 We never play tennis.
3 Mum sometimes watches TV. 4 He is always late for school.
5 My cat often sleeps on my bed.

Exercise 5
1 past 2 is 3 minutes 4 at 5 clock

Unit 7

Exercise 1
1 hamster 2 iguana 3 parrot 4 goldfish 5 rabbit

Exercise 2
1 a fast bird 2 a dangerous lion 3 a slow tortoise 4 an ugly frog
5 a strong elephant

Exercise 3
1 doesn't sing 2 don't live 3 doesn't like 4 don't speak 5 don't want

Exercise 4
1 Does Tom wear jeans to school? 2 No, he doesn't. 3 Do your friends like football?
4 Yes, they do. 5 Does your granny visit you every week?

Exercise 5
1 you 2 have 3 please 4 that's 5 are

Unit 8

Exercise 1
1 taekwondo 2 ice-skating 3 January 4 autumn 5 early

Exercise 2
1 brush 2 play 3 go 4 drink 5 fruit

Exercise 3
1 My sister doesn't like roller skating. 2 Do you like swimming? 3 I love singing.
4 We don't like getting up early. 5 Do your friends like eating pizza?

Exercise 4
1 Where 2 How 3 them 4 her 5 it

Exercise 5
1 like 2 It's 3 it 4 is 5 Me